THE SHORTEST HISTORY OF ECONOMICS

Other Titles in the Shortest History Series

The Shortest History of India by John Zubrzycki
The Shortest History of Democracy by John Keane
The Shortest History of China by Linda Jaivin
The Shortest History of the Soviet Union by Sheila Fitzpatrick
The Shortest History of the Crown by Stephen Bates
The Shortest History of the Universe by David Baker
The Shortest History of War by Gwynne Dyer
The Shortest History of Israel and Palestine by Michael Scott-Baumann

Also by Andrew Leigh

What's the Worst That Could Happen? Existential Risk and Extreme Politics (2021)
Reconnected: A Community Builder' Handbook (2020)
Innovation + Equality: How to Create a Future That Is More Star Trek Than Terminator (2019)
Randomistas: How Radical Researchers Are Changing Our World (2018)
Choosing Openness (2017)
The Economics of Just About Everything: The Hidden Reasons for Our Curious Choices and Surprising Successes (2014)
The Luck of Politics: True Tales of Disaster and Outrageous Fortune (2014)
Battlers and Billionairs: The Story of Inequality in Australia (2013)

THE SHORTEST HISTORY OF ECONOMICS

ANDREW LEIGH

PICADOR INDIA

First published in Black Inc., Australia
First published in India 2024 by Picador India
an imprint of Pan Macmillan Publishing India Private Limited
707 Kailash Building
26 K. G. Marg, New Delhi 110001
www.panmacmillan.co.in

Pan Macmillan, The Smithson, 6 Briset Street, Farringdon, London EC1M 5NR
Associated companies throughout the world
www.panmacmillan.com

ISBN 978-81-19300-90-7

7 9 8 6

Printed and bound in India by Thomson Press India Ltd.

FSC www.fsc.org MIX Paper | Supporting responsible forestry FSC® C010615

Contents

Introduction

IN PREHISTORIC TIMES, THE ONLY source of artificial light was a wood fire. To produce as much light as a regular household lightbulb now gives off in an hour would have taken our prehistoric ancestors fifty-eight hours of foraging for timber.[1] By Babylonian times, the best lighting technology was a lamp that burned sesame oil. To produce the same amount of light, a Babylonian worker in around 1750 BCE would have had to work for forty-one hours.

An earthenware lamp, which used a cotton wick and oil or ghee.

Then came candles. Initially made from animal fat, they were time-consuming to produce (and smelt awful). Even in the late 1700s, the typical worker would have to devote five hours' work to producing candles that emitted as much light as a regular household lightbulb gives off in an hour. Through the 1800s came developments in gas lamps, which reduced the time cost of an hour of light to a few hours of work.

With the invention of the electric bulb, light got cheaper still. By the early 1900s, it took just minutes of work to buy an hour of light. Today, less than one second of work will earn you enough money to run a modern household lightbulb for an hour. Measured in terms of artificial light, the earnings from work are 300,000 times higher today than they were in prehistoric times, and 30,000 times higher than they were in 1800. Where our ancient ancestors once toiled to brighten their nights, we rarely even think about the cost as we flick on a light.

The progression of lighting technology: a candle, incandescent bulb, fluorescent bulb and LED bulb.

Two forces have driven this remarkable change. Lighting technologies are better (and still improving by the day). And workers are more productive, which means that we earn more in an hour than our ancestors did.

The history of light illuminates some key themes of this book. Where prehistoric people had to do everything, modern workers specialise in what we do best. Markets allow us to exchange our output with that of other people. Prices create incentives to produce more when there's a shortage and less when there's a glut. Yet the market system is far from perfect. Unemployment, cartels, traffic congestion, overfishing and pollution are just a few of the problems that emerge when markets fail.

This small book tells a big story. It is the story of capitalism – of how our market system developed. It is the story of the discipline of economics, and some of the key figures who formed it. And it is the story of how economic forces have shaped world history. Why didn't Africa colonise Europe instead of the other way around? What happened when countries erected trade and immigration barriers in the 1930s? Why did the Allies win World War II? Why did inequality in many advanced countries fall during the 1950s and 1960s? How did property rights drive China's growth surge in the 1980s? How does climate change threaten our future prosperity? You'll find answers to these questions and more in this book.

Economics can be defined as a social science that studies how people maximise their wellbeing in the face of scarcity.

It considers the behaviour of people as individuals, and how we work together in households and corporations. It focuses on how we interact in markets, in which buyers and sellers together determine the equilibrium price. Economics also considers what happens when markets fail, and how public policy might ameliorate poverty, climate change or price-fixing.

This is a story that blends microeconomics and macroeconomics.[2] Microeconomics is the study of how individuals make decisions. Macroeconomics looks at the economy as a whole. Too often, popular books about economics focus on one or the other. *Freakonomics*, *Discover Your Inner Economist* and *50 Things That Made the Modern Economy* introduce the reader to microeconomics. *The Return of Depression Economics*, *Slouching Towards Utopia* and *This Time Is Different* help explain macroeconomics. This book synthesises both perspectives. We'll move chronologically through history, touching on the decisions of individuals and the trajectory of entire societies.

Critics who think economics is bleak, moneygrubbing or narrow-minded like to quote Thomas Carlyle's description of the discipline as 'the dismal science', ignoring where the criticism comes from. Carlyle, who was writing in the 1800s, was a racist who believed that slavery should be reintroduced in the West Indies. The 'dismal' view Carlyle was attacking was that all people are equal. Like many economists, I wear the insult with pride.

Carlyle also disparagingly said, 'Teach a parrot the terms supply and demand and you've got an economist.'[3] Supply and demand graphs can be handy, but you won't find them in this book. And you certainly don't need to have studied any economics to enjoy the stories that follow. Learning to think like an economist can change your life for the better. The secret of our discipline is that the most powerful insights come from a handful of big ideas that anyone can comprehend.

I've mentioned one of these ideas already: incentives. In sporting contests where there's a big first prize and a small second prize, performance improves. Runners go faster. Golfers finish in fewer shots.[4] Incentives can even affect when we're born. When Australia introduced a 'baby bonus' for children born on or after 1 July 2004, that day set a record for the number of births.[5] Why? Because expectant mothers delayed induction procedures and caesarean section operations to get the financial reward. When the United States changed inheritance tax rates, the timing of deaths shifted too: indicating that a small number of people died later (or earlier) to minimise their tax bill.[6] There's a cliché that nothing in life is certain except death and taxes. In this case, tax rates changed, and death rates followed.

That's not to say that economics is all about greed. Elinor Ostrom, the first woman to win the Nobel Prize in economics, found many contexts – from fisheries in Indonesia to forests in Nepal – in which people cooperated to manage scarce resources. In her Nobel Prize lecture, Ostrom criticised the tendency of economists to design institutions for entirely self-interested individuals. Instead, she argued, 'a core goal of public policy should be to facilitate the development of institutions that bring out the best in humans'. Incentives matter, but I'll endeavour to capture Ostrom's optimism, and show that economists can be idealists too.

Another big idea of economics is specialisation. How many of us can provide a good haircut, replace a broken car windscreen, turn grapes into wine, or write a smartphone app? Given a few months, most people could learn to do each of these tasks with some level of proficiency, but unless you'd enjoy the experience, a better approach is to pay an expert, and focus instead on what you do best. If you spent your life aiming to become reasonably good at everything, you'd probably end up as the human equivalent of a Swiss Army knife – with a finicky knife, annoyingly tiny scissors and an impractical screwdriver. Job specialisation is one of the keys to the modern economy.

The process of making things has become specialised too. For example, some Chinese cities have become expert in making a single kind of product. Yiwu produces most of the world's Christmas decorations. Huludao makes a quarter of the world's swimwear. Danyang is known as 'spectacles city'. Taizhou, which has long specialised in bathroom products, has now become a global centre for innovation in intelligent toilets.[7]

As specialisation flourishes, trade becomes invaluable. Boeing's 787 Dreamliner includes batteries from Japan, wing tips from South Korea, floor beams from India, horizontal stabilisers from Italy, landing gear from France, cargo doors from Sweden and thrust reversers from Mexico.[8] A typical smartphone could most accurately be labelled 'Made in the World'. By sourcing components and raw materials from the lowest-cost suppliers, it becomes possible to create items that would be unaffordable if they had to be built using only local materials.

Perhaps the most powerful illustration of specialisation came when designer Thomas Thwaites decided to make a toaster from scratch – using only his own labour and raw materials he had personally sourced.[9] Thwaites obtained iron ore from a disused mine in England, copper from a mine in Wales, and mica from a mountain in Scotland. When a home blast furnace failed to make steel, he resorted to smelting iron ore in his microwave. The plastic casing came from melting down garbage. In the end, Thwaites's toaster experiment took nine months. If we value his time at the average wage in the United Kingdom at the time, the labour cost was £19,000, plus around £1000 for expenses.[10] Thwaites's £20,000 toaster was about 5000 times costlier than if he had bought one at his local retailer for £4. Oh, and store-bought toasters actually work. When Thwaites plugged his toaster in, it lasted five seconds before it began melting down.

Another principle of economics is that big events are rarely driven by sudden shifts in norms or culture. More often, dramatic changes are due to new technologies or changing policies. If you want to understand why international trade boomed in the post-war decades, it helps to know about the invention of the standardised shipping container in 1956 and the reduction in global tariffs through successive rounds of world trade talks. If you want to know why basketball games today are more exciting than half a century ago, consider the role of the shot clock and the three-point rule. This book seeks to unearth the hidden economic forces behind wars, religious movements and social transformations.

The story of economics starts with the agricultural revolution that saw communities move from hunter-gatherer tribes to create the civilisations of Ancient Egypt, Greece and Rome. Trade between regions was enabled by water-borne transport. China's Grand Canal connected provinces. The age of sail connected Europe, Africa and the Americas – transporting agricultural products, manufactured goods and enslaved people in a highly profitable triangular trade.

The next major revolution was the industrial revolution, which kickstarted manufacturing and turbocharged economic growth. Alongside the new gadgets came intellectual breakthroughs, as the discipline of economics took shape. By the early 1900s, the innovation of the assembly line saw cars produced at ever-decreasing prices, and globalisation knitted the world together like never before. Two world wars and the Great Depression broke many of those connections, destroying lives, livelihoods and linkages.

For many in the advanced world, the post-war era was a period of shared prosperity, but growth was patchier elsewhere. In China, the early decades of communist rule were marked by capricious policies that undermined growth until the country's market turned in 1978. In India, the big change came in 1990. Growth across much of Asia saw a growing divergence between living standards in that region and those in slower-growing Africa. By the beginning of the twenty-first century, inequality within many countries had risen sharply.

Much of economics is now focused on questions of market failure. A great deal of competition policy is motivated by curtailing monopoly power. A central concern of the macroeconomics pioneered by John Maynard Keynes is reducing unemployment. Climate policy addresses the market failure that means pollution can be profitable for companies, but ruinous for the planet. Similarly, behavioural economics acknowledges that humans do not always behave like cool, calculating happiness-maximising machines, but tend to deviate in systematic ways from the rational rule. As the discipline of economics has evolved, both theory and data have allowed researchers to build better models of human behaviour, making economics more interesting and more useful.

But before we get to *Homo economicus*, we must start at the beginning, with the way that economics shaped our species, *Homo sapiens*.

1

OUT OF AFRICA AND INTO AGRICULTURE

MODERN HUMANS EVOLVED IN SOUTHERN Africa around 300,000 years ago.[1] Our ancient ancestors had language, art and dance, raised children in family units and told stories. Around 65,000 years ago, they invented spears and bows for hunting, needles for sewing and boats for travelling.[2] Unlike earlier primates, their capacity for language and abstract thought allowed *Homo sapiens* to engage in collective learning: building a shared knowledge base that exceeded the capacity of any individual person.[3] But their lives largely remained nomadic: hunting animals and feeding on local plants, then moving on when the resources were gone.

Early societies differed in providing for those who could not work. Some prehistoric societies show evidence of caring for the elderly – carving canes so they could walk and chewing food for those whose teeth no longer worked. Other hunter-gatherer societies – especially the ones that moved long distances – tended to kill or abandon those who were elderly or disabled, lest they endanger the whole group's prospects.

So what was life like for most people in this era? 'Nothing is more gentle than man in his primitive state,' wrote Swiss philosopher Jean-Jacques Rousseau. His English counterpart Thomas Hobbes took an utterly different view, declaring that early human life was 'solitary, poor, nasty, brutish, and short'.

Thanks to forensic archaeology (sometimes dubbed 'CSI Palaeolithic'), modern researchers have been able to glean a great deal about life in this era. They estimate that two-fifths of babies did not live to see their first birthday. Life expectancy was around thirty-three years.[4] Violence was ever-present – from competitors in your own tribe and attackers from neighbouring groups. Up to 15 per cent of people in nomadic societies died a violent death.[5] Before the age of farming, most people would have shivered through winter, and gone to bed with growling stomachs. Hobbes was right. Rousseau was wrong.

Settled agriculture has no single origin point, but one of the 'firsts' took place in northwestern India. The town of Kalibangan, about three hours' drive from the border with Pakistan, was once the confluence of two rivers. It is home to one of the world's major archaeological sites: the oldest ploughed field. Here, furrows are ploughed both north–south and east–west, suggesting that two crops were grown together – perhaps cereals and mustard.[6]

Kalibangan was a major city in the Indus Valley civilisation, which prospered from 3300 to 1300 BCE. Farming allowed people to settle and build more comfortable homes – some even had flush toilets. Their builders hit upon the ideal brick size: the dimensional ratio of 1:2:4 that is still in use today.[7] Adults wielded bronze tools and played dice games. Archaeologists have unearthed children's toys such as whistles and spinning tops. In contrast with nomadic living, settled agriculture provided the environment in which tools and toys could be made and used.

The agricultural revolution spurred the Indus Valley civilisation to trade with others. To move goods across land, its citizens built carts – possibly the first use of wheeled transport in history. Their cities were laid out in a grid pattern, just as many modern cities are today. They built boats and dredged a canal. Indus Valley traders brought back raw materials such as jade from China, cedar wood from the Himalayas and lapis lazuli from Afghanistan. In return, they sold jewellery, pottery and metal tools.

At its peak, the Indus Valley civilisation had a population of around 5 million people.[8] Yet it remained undiscovered by archaeologists until the 1920s. A major reason for this is that the civilisation was relatively equal. Ancient Egyptians built the pyramids, Ancient Greeks built the Acropolis, and Ancient Romans built the Pantheon. Big edifices were typically a marker of vast differences in wealth and power – what one scholar has called the 'monumental problem'.[9] By contrast, the Indus Valley civilisation constructed few monuments. At the time, this served their people well, but it meant that Indus Valley cities remained unseen for over 2,000 years after the area's rivers dried up.

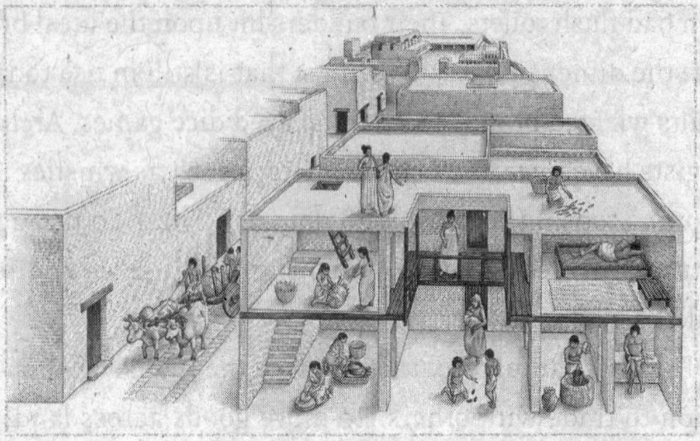

The Indus Valley civilisation did not build the kinds of monuments that signified wealth inequality in other civilisations.

Farming marked a turning point for the world economy because it allowed communities to build up a surplus. Storing food enabled people to eat well all year round. It also provided an early form of insurance against famine if the harvest failed. When people's consumption is less volatile than their incomes, economists say that they are 'consumption smoothing'. Consumption smoothing explains why many people in modern economies borrow to buy a home, save for retirement and take out health insurance. The uncertainty that plagued people's lives in prehistoric times must have been extremely stressful for many citizens. Even today, the working poor in advanced countries suffer from large swings in income from month to month, causing considerable anxiety and making it hard to plan for the future.

In a few places, food was plentiful enough that hunter-gatherers could live a fulfilling life. On the western edge of the

Kalahari Desert live a group of people called the !Kung (the exclamation point is pronounced with a click of the tongue). The area has many mongongo trees, whose nuts are high in protein and fat, and can be stored for long periods. Traditionally, the average !Kung ate around 300 nuts a day, providing about one-third of their energy intake. As one member of the !Kung told a visitor, 'Why should we plant [crops] when there are so many mongongo nuts in the world?'[10] But the !Kung are the exception. In most of the world, farming meant that people could consume more calories and be more certain about where their next meal would come from.

The Levant, an area bordering the eastern edge of the Mediterranean Sea, was especially promising for farmers. Following the end of the last ice age, the Levant experienced several long dry periods, which prompted societies to experiment with farming. From 10,000 to 8000 BCE, farmers bred crops by selecting those with larger seeds and a less bitter taste. The Levant, part of what is sometimes called 'the fertile crescent', happened to have several plant species that could be domesticated (adapted for human use). These eight 'founder crops' – emmer wheat, einkorn wheat, hulled barley, peas, lentils, bitter vetch, chickpeas and flax – were essential to the development of agriculture.[11] Early farmers developed flint knives and grindstones to assist with harvesting and processing. Societies moved from being nomadic communities to having settlements built around agriculture.

The most important invention that enabled agriculture was the plough. Breaking up the earth makes planting easier, brings up fresh soil nutrients, and buries weeds. Early farmers did this using sticks and hoes: not all that different from the way you might till the soil in a backyard vegetable plot today. But the plough made it possible to use the energy of animals to turn the soil.

Early Egyptian ploughs were scratch ploughs, akin to a stick being pulled through the earth. During the Qin and Han dynasties (221 BCE to 220 CE), Chinese farmers developed the turn plough, which turns the soil upside down, creating furrows.[12] Settled agriculture was five or six times more productive than foraging.[13] The plough brought the end of a society in which everyone's occupation was effectively 'food finder'. Indeed, one historian has argued that the entire modern world is the result of the plough.[14]

Ploughs changed power dynamics too. Digging stick agriculture is relatively gender-equal, but ploughs require significant upper body strength to pull the plough or control the animal that pulls it. So the plough made farming a more male-dominated activity. The legacy of this technology has echoed down the generations.[15] In countries where plough use was uncommon (such as Rwanda and Madagascar), gender norms are more equal than in countries where plough use was common (such as Mauritania and Ethiopia). Even among immigrants who have recently moved to advanced countries, those from countries with a heritage of plough use are less likely to believe that women should have jobs outside the home.

Some regions of the world were more amenable to farming than others. Eurasia happened to have plant and animal species that were well suited to domestication. As we have seen, Eurasia's native plants included variants of barley, wheat and legumes, which could be stored for months. Other regions had bananas and yams, which spoiled in days. With animals, it was a similar story. Eurasia had goats, sheep and cattle, which could be used for meat, milk and hides. By contrast, African zebras and Australian kangaroos are harder to tame.

The shape of the continents mattered too. Where Eurasia is wide, Africa and the Americas are long. This means that people could explore (and exploit) Eurasia while staying in the same climatic band. Eurasia's east–west explorers did not have to develop new ways of surviving in an unfamiliar environment, and their farming innovations could spread across similar climates. But adventurers in Africa and the Americas had the more arduous task of travelling north–south. As geographer Jared Diamond notes, these initial coincidences explain why Eurasia colonised Africa, the Americas and Oceania,

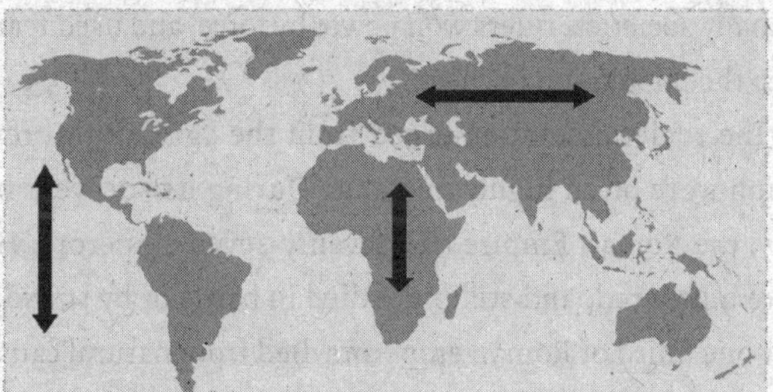

It was easier to migrate within similar climates (east to west) than varied climates (north to south).

rather than the other way around. Because wealth ultimately fuelled military might, bigger agricultural revolutions laid the groundwork for empire-building.

In theory, the agricultural revolution could have made everyone better off. Because farming was more efficient than hunting and gathering, it did not require the labour of everyone in the society. For the first time, that opened the possibility for people to specialise as craftspeople and builders. Farming enabled cities, where people invented new tools and traded in flourishing markets. The Indus Valley civilisation might be the best example in history of a community where settled agriculture led to shared prosperity.

Unfortunately, the agricultural revolution also created the potential for less benign rulers to emerge. Hunter-gatherers were mobile, which meant that nobody owned much property. By contrast, farming created surpluses. This made it possible for leaders to enrich themselves and their families, extracting resources from the population to fund a repressive army. In many societies, rulers won power by force, and used fear to keep the population in check.

The societies that emerged from the agricultural revolution were often highly unstable. During its 500-year history, the Roman Empire had seventy-seven emperors. Half were murdered, and still more died in battle or by suicide.[16] Just one-third of Roman emperors died from natural causes. In one exceptionally brutal eighteen-month period, Nero died by suicide, Galba was murdered, Otho died by suicide and Vitellius was murdered. On the battlefield, war was sometimes fought *Bellum Romanum* – an all-out approach that involved destroying crops, raping women and enslaving or executing captives. The victims of the Roman Empire's brutal expansion probably thought that they would have been better off without the agricultural revolution.

Another unexpected downside of settled agriculture was that diets tended to be less diverse. Hunter-gatherers consumed a broad range of berries, nuts and animals, while people in farming communities often got most of their calories from just a few starchy plants. One study, based on examining skeletal remains before and after the agricultural revolution, estimates that average heights dropped by about 10 centimetres (4 inches).[17] Hobbes was right that life was 'short' in the state of nature, but the initial effect of the agricultural revolution was a shorter population.

At first, the agricultural revolution increased rates of malnutrition, crowded people into disease-ridden cities and worsened inequality. Yet it also enabled innovators, who ultimately laid the foundation for people to have longer and more enjoyable lives than those of our stone age ancestors.[18] Just as agriculture created the potential for capricious dictators to arise, it also produced an environment in which people could think about improving themselves and the world around them.

An intellectual elite had time to tinker with ideas, build models and develop fresh ways of engaging with the world. Ancient Mesopotamia made breakthroughs in mathematics, maps, writing and sailboats. Ancient Egypt innovated in art, writing and architecture. The Mayan civilisation made discoveries in astronomy and record-keeping. The Ancient Greeks achieved advances in science, technology, literature and democracy. There was even an early welfare state. From 98 to 272 CE, Rome had a program known as the *alimenta*, which provided food and subsidised education to orphans and poor children. But it helped only a fraction of those in need, and was terminated by Emperor Aurelian.

Where a society put its inventive energies varied enormously. To construct the Great Pyramid of Giza around 2600 BCE required use of trigonometry and Pythagoras' theorem. It remained the world's tallest building for the next 3,800 years. Yet Ancient Egyptians did not invent the wheel – they relied instead on tens of thousands of workers, who hauled stone blocks from quarries on sledges. The rulers of Ancient Rome built aqueducts and beautiful high-domed buildings. Yet they did not widely adopt the waterwheel or the windmill, and it was not until after the fall of the Roman Empire that watermills became commonplace across Europe.[19]

Why didn't the remarkable thinkers of this era pay more attention to labour-saving devices? Economics provides an answer. When labour costs are low, there is less incentive to invest in technologies that make workers more efficient. In our modern era, European restaurants invested in electronic ordering systems decades before restaurants in the United States. The reason was simple: hiring waitstaff is costlier in Europe, so firms have an incentive to make them as productive as possible.

THE ECONOMICS OF RELIGION

The period of classical antiquity saw the start of the three Abrahamic religions: Judaism, Christianity and Islam. One reason for their rise goes back to a key insight from economics: that competition benefits consumers, by encouraging greater innovation. So it is no coincidence that these faiths emerged in an era of intense religious competition.

The same forces shape religion in the modern age. Churchgoing rates are higher in North America (with robust competition between denominations) than in Scandinavian countries (where churches often have a government-granted monopoly). Noting the relationship between diversity and religiosity, former US president Thomas Jefferson quipped that in matters of religion, the maxim should be 'Divided we stand, united, we fall.'[20]

When it comes to religion, competition boosts participation.

Economists also observe that the strict requirements of many religions – including restrictions on food, clothing and social mixing – have an economic purpose. Without such rules, it would be easy for outsiders to slip into the group and enjoy its benefits without paying the cost. Five out of six people in the world today are religious.[21] Over the lifecycle, people tend to become less religious, but because religious parents have more children, the world is projected to become more religious over the coming decades. Theologically moderate religions tend to have more lapsed members, while theologically conservative religions tend to have the highest birthrates. Thus the fastest-growing religions tend to be those with the strictest doctrines.

Likewise, when the innovators of Ancient Egypt and Ancient Rome were considering the most pressing technology problems, they did so in a society where much of the work was carried out by enslaved people. With so many in bondage, the ruling class didn't have much interest in raising the output of the enslaved class. Slavery in the Ancient world wasn't just morally wrong – it also reduced the incentive to make people more productive.

Similar issues arose in Ancient China, where an abundance of workers muted the incentive to exploit new innovations. The Chinese were well ahead of their European counterparts in the manufacture of silk cloth, the production of items made of bronze and steel, and the use of paper for writing. The magnetic compass was invented in China around the fourth to the second century BCE. Yet these inventions did not transform the economy in the ways that might have been expected. In Ancient China, aristocrats dominated the ruling elite, and the prevailing view was one of disdain for merchants and commerce. As a result, innovations in metalwork were largely in weapons and artworks, not practical tools.[22] The invention of the compass did not turn China into a leading maritime power. Economic success requires more than inventions. It also takes the right institutions for inventions to change lives.

One invention that emerged in many ancient societies was money. Money has three qualities. First, it is a unit of account, providing a common language to express the value of different items. Rather than saying that two cows are worth one axe, we can say that both are worth one silver coin.

Second, it is a store of value, allowing wealth to be held in a form that does not rot or die. Third, it is a medium of exchange, simplifying commerce between people who might want to buy two cows, but don't have an axe to offer in exchange.

Money emerged in different forms. In Ancient Greece, coins were produced between 700 and 600 BCE, and came to be known as *drachma*, meaning 'a handful'.[23] In the Ancient Olympics, winners received prizes of up to 1,000 drachma to accompany their olive wreaths.[24] The Romans were relatively late in producing currency, but when they began making silver coins in 269 BCE near the temple of Juno Moneta, some bore the word 'Moneta', which gave us the word money.

Coins provided a straightforward way to pay for daily items. Coins could be carried in a pouch while travelling. They were an essential aspect of the sprawling Roman Empire. Sometimes the first people knew of a new emperor was when they saw his image on a coin.

But coins are not the only possible form of money. On the Yap islands in Micronesia, stone sculptures were used as money. The largest of these stones was 3.6 metres (12 feet) in diameter. It was not moved when it changed ownership – instead the Yapese kept the stone in place and everyone in the community took note of the new owner. This made large stone sculptures inconvenient for commerce, but it is not as unusual as it sounds. In modern times, central banks sometimes hold gold in their vaults. When the gold is sold, it often involves just a change in an electronic ledger, without the physical gold moving at all. The Yapese would appreciate it.

Yapese stones made from carved limestone.

Whether in the form of sculptures or coins, a common feature of money in this era was that it had inherent value. In some cases, merchants would issue promissory notes to one another, but money was made of something precious. This would change around 1000 CE, when the Chinese government became the first in the world to issue paper money – inherently worthless pieces of paper that represented a promise of value.

Another aspect of economic development was the increase in trade volumes between regions. As we have seen in the case of the Indus Valley civilisation, specialisation within a society led to the production of new goods, such as clothes and tools. That in turn led to specialisation between societies, which is the basis for trade. When one society is comparatively better at producing a product or service, then it can potentially benefit from trade.

Wait, why did I write *comparatively* better, rather than just better? To see this, let's go back to specialisation in the workforce. Suppose that the best pottery maker in the village is also the best baker. Now imagine that she is ten times better than the next person at pottery, but only twice as good at baking. In this example, the output of the community will be greatest if she spends all her time doing pottery, and buys her bread from someone else.

What holds for our master potter also applies to countries, cities and regions. Imagine that Ancient China produced both silk and gold more cheaply than Ancient Rome, but that the Chinese were ten times more efficient at producing silk, and only twice as efficient at mining gold. In that case, it might make sense for China to export silk and import gold. Trade along the Silk Road depended only on *comparative* advantage, not absolute advantage. Even a country that produces everything more efficiently than its neighbours can gain from trade.

Yet there's a reason that even modern societies do not import heavy, low-value products such as gravel. When the cost of transport is high, relative to the value of the products being moved, trade becomes uneconomic. Even after the invention of the wheel, the poor quality of most roads meant that it was usually easier to strap loads onto the backs of horses and camels than to move them on carts. Consequently, most land trade was confined to products such as wine, olive oil, precious stones, valuable metals and rare spices. Around 300 CE, the price of a wagonload of wheat doubled if it was transported 500 kilometres (about 300 miles).[25]

2

THE GRAND CANAL, THE PRINTING PRESS AND THE PLAGUE

GIVEN THAT WATER COVERS MORE than two-thirds of our planet's surface, the planet should perhaps be called 'water' rather than 'earth'. For millennia, humans have travelled by water, in boats powered by oars, sails or both. Moving goods on water was cheaper than transporting them by land. This made rivers and oceans more important to commerce than roads. Chinese rulers in the Sui dynasty (581 to 618 CE) built the Grand Canal, the longest canal or artificial river in the world. At more than 1,600 kilometres (1,000 miles) in length, it connects the Yellow River and the Yangtse River. The original impetus for constructing the canal was so that the government in Beijing could collect grain levied as taxes.[1]

But the canal also helped spur trade between provinces, and contributed to the economic engagement and cosmopolitan openness that saw China thrive during the Tang dynasty (618 to 907 CE). The closure of the Grand Canal in the 1800s caused economic hardship and social unrest in surrounding provinces, reflecting how important it was.[2] The Grand Canal is less famous than the Great Wall, but it was more significant economically. The construction of the Grand Canal boosted prosperity, encouraged travel and improved political stability. By the year 1000 CE, Chinese living standards were higher than in England; converted into today's currency, the average daily income per person was US$3.36 in China, compared with US$3.15 in England.[3]

Around the world, the importance of water travel meant that the most successful cities were by the coast, ideally with deep-water ports that allowed ships to shelter from a storm. Lisbon, Alexandria and Athens were among the cities that prospered in the golden age of maritime transport. Port cities became financial centres. In Genoa, moneychangers stored the coins of merchants, settled debts by moving money between accounts, and provided loans to finance new voyages.[4]

In Venice, a novel form of risk sharing called the *colleganza* allowed poorer merchants to finance sea voyages by agreeing to share the profits with investors.[5] The system created a pathway to upward mobility for merchants, and by the early 1300s, Venice was a world banking centre. Then Venice's established families closed the *colleganza* off to commoners, entrenching their position at the top of the economic hierarchy. Patronage replaced merit. Venice lost its position as a leader in global commerce, and suffered a series of military defeats. Innovation and egalitarianism were replaced by insider cronyism – and Venetians were poorer for it.

SOCIAL MOBILITY

Under China's ancient fēngjiàn system, India's traditional caste system and European medieval feudalism, a person's position in society was determined from birth. Mobility across generations was limited, because a child's social status was a function of their parents' status.

Most people in modern capitalist societies are appalled by such a rigid class system. People across the ideological spectrum prize social mobility – the idea that anyone can 'make it'. Yet in practice, countries differ considerably in the degree to which children's outcomes are related to those of their parents. The highest levels of mobility tend to be found in Scandinavia, while the lowest are in Latin America.

One reason for this is that inequality (the gap between rich and poor) is strongly related to mobility (the relationship between incomes of parent and child). We can think of this using the analogy of a ladder, with inequality represented as the gap between the rungs, and mobility as the chance that someone climbs up or down. When the rungs are further apart, less climbing takes place. This has become known as 'the Great Gatsby Curve'.[6] Because Latin America is more unequal than Scandinavia, it is also less mobile.

Until now, we've been discussing social mobility across a single generation. But another approach makes it possible to look across multiple generations, to test for the persistence of dynasties. To understand long-term patterns of social mobility, economist Gregory Clark uses rare surnames to test whether societies are fluid or static.[7] Take the case of Samuel Pepys (1633–1703), the diarist who served as secretary of the English Admiralty. In the past five centuries, people with the surname Pepys have attended Oxford and Cambridge universities at a rate at least twenty times that of the general population. Where we can observe the value of their estates, Pepyses left wealth at least five times the British average. Only in a society with extremely low levels of social mobility would we expect a name to persist among the elites in this way.

Rare elite surnames endure in other countries too. United States tax authorities reported the names of top income earners in the early 1920s. A century later, people with those surnames are three to four times as likely to be doctors or lawyers. United States residents with the high-status surname Katz, for example, are six times as likely to be doctors and lawyers.

In Japan, samurai surnames date back to before the 1868 Meiji Restoration. In the modern age, they are overrepresented at least fourfold among doctors, lawyers and scholarly authors. In China, Qing surnames overrepresented among the nineteenth-century elite are also overrepresented among contemporary corporate board chairs and government officials.

In Chile, surnames overrepresented among landowners in the 1850s are still overrepresented among high-earning occupations. In Sweden, a set of 'noble surnames' were created in the 1600s and 1700s. In the current era, those names have twice their expected share of doctors and five times their expected share of lawyers. Social status is remarkably persistent, even over ten generations.

Another city whose fortune was shaped by the shipping trade was Bruges, located on the Zwin estuary. The city was so affluent in 1301 that when the Queen of France visited, she remarked, 'I thought I alone was queen, but I see that I have six hundred rivals here.'[8] Two centuries later, when the Zwin estuary silted up, Bruges's economy withered. The region's commercial centre moved 80 kilometres (50 miles) west, to Antwerp, where ships could dock easily. Eventually, wits dubbed the city 'Bruges-La-Morte'.

Trade and migration were at their most valuable when they brought new ideas, and products that could be replicated. Reading glasses were invented in Italy around 1290, and quickly spread across Europe. Traders brought maize to China in the 1300s (and later, sweet potatoes), providing staple food sources in regions that did not get enough rainfall to sustain rice; this led to rapid population growth in the ensuing centuries.[9] The moveable-type printing press was invented in Germany around 1440, and kickstarted the printing revolution. More books were produced in the next fifty years than had been produced in the previous thousand years.[10]

Economists describe physical goods as 'rivalrous' and ideas as 'non-rivalrous'. When I hand over three apples to you, I no longer have three apples. But if I teach you to juggle apples, then we both share the fun (particularly if we don't mind eating bruised apples). The idea of non-rivalry is essential to how economists think about innovation. In the case of reading glasses and the printing press, neither innovation was protected by intellectual property laws. This was a boon for consumers because it meant that others could copy, adapt and improve them. But the ability to freely copy reduced the incentive to invent. Over the coming centuries – starting with Venice's patent statute of 1474 – countries put in place patent laws, which gave inventors a temporary monopoly in exchange for sharing their idea.

The dispersion of knowledge also got a boost from one of the key social changes of this period: the Reformation. When Martin Luther and his followers split off from the Catholic Church, they encouraged their adherents to read the Bible for themselves. This boosted literacy levels and fuelled economic development in Protestant areas of Germany. Indeed, even in modern-day Germany – 500 years after Luther – Protestants tend to be more educated and have higher incomes.[11]

In the Middle Ages – the period from the fifth to the fifteenth century – religion also affected economic development in other ways. Tight bonds of trust among Jewish communities made them ideally placed to succeed in the moneylending and money-transfer business, which was both profitable and stigmatised. From its inception in 610 CE, Islam was closely connected to trade (Mohammed was a merchant), and trust between Muslims helped to increase commerce in Islamic communities.[12] Economics also helps explain religious wars. The First Crusade (1096–1099) can be seen as an attempt by the Catholic Church to expand its monopoly over new territories.[13]

During the Middle Ages, many in Europe lived under feudalism, a system in which land was owned by the lords and farmed by the peasantry. In effect, peasants fed the nobility in exchange for protection against bandits. There were few chances to move up the hierarchy, and the clergy maintained the social order.

It was not uncommon for artisans to literally carve their prices in stone on the wall, knowing that their rates would not change much from one generation to the next. There were some technological changes (such as the proliferation of watermills we noted earlier), but life remained tough. Even by the end of the Middle Ages, most people would have eaten a plain diet, with only occasional meat and fish to supplement unappetising stews and unvarying starchy grains. There were no printed books, most homes had little furniture, and no one had running water. An infected scratch could lead to death, and illness was common. One in three babies died before their first birthday, and childbirth claimed the life of one-third of mothers.[14]

The worst bacteria was *yersinia pestis*, dubbed the Black Death. The bubonic plague originated in Central Asia and was brought to Europe in 1347 by Genoese traders sailing from the Black Sea. It killed around one-third of Europe's population – a higher toll than even the most brutal wars. In Cairo, it killed half the population. Muslims making the hajj brought the disease to Mecca in 1349. In cities, proximity accelerated the spread of the disease, so people fled to the countryside. Among the most famous is Giovanni Boccaccio, who fled Florence – a city where up to three-quarters of the population died – to write his masterpiece *The Decameron*. From 1300 to 1400, the world population shrank from 430 million to 350 million.

The Black Death also provides a dramatic illustration of economics in action.[15] A scarcity of workers doubled European real wages (that is, wages after inflation). Suddenly land was relatively abundant, so rents declined. This helped shift the power balance in favour of peasants and against landowners. To a large extent, the plague killed feudalism. The Black Death also affected prices. Simple foodstuffs such as wheat became cheaper. Manufactured goods that required a lot of labour became more expensive. With wages rising and land rents falling, farmers shifted their production towards land-intensive agriculture, such as cattle and sheep farming. Responding to the increase in their incomes, workers started to eat more meat. There was a growing demand for beer, a marker of living standards in this era.

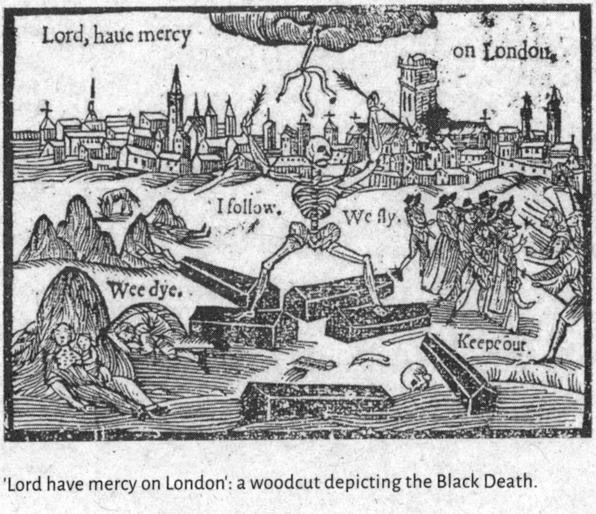

'Lord have mercy on London': a woodcut depicting the Black Death.

Growth in Europe may have been slow by today's standards, but by the 1400s, it was the most affluent region of the globe. As we have seen, Europe's success was rooted in luck. Compared with Africa and the Americas, Eurasia had more domesticable plants and animals, and its wide geography allowed people to range further while staying in the same climatic band.

3

THE AGE OF SAIL

THE RELATIVE PROSPERITY OF EUROPE funded steady improvements in maritime technology. The ships of this era were three-masted or 'full-rigged', had sturdier hulls, and used rudders instead of steering oars. Advances in sails made it possible to tack into the wind. Bigger ships could make longer voyages. Better compasses, maps and understanding of wind patterns allowed ships to follow the fastest routes. The invention of the sea astrolabe allowed sailors to figure out their latitude.

Still, there was plenty that early explorers didn't know. When Christopher Columbus sailed across the Atlantic in 1492, he was expecting to reach India and China, not the Americas (the inaccurate naming of the West Indies reflects this mistake). Other major expeditions followed. In 1498, Vasco da Gama established a sea route to India. In 1519, Ferdinand Magellan began an expedition that would be the first to circumnavigate the globe (though Magellan himself did not make it home, dying in a battle in the Philippines). Economics was at the heart of these expeditions – explorers sought to fund their journeys with new products, new markets and new land.

Discovering new countries and lowering the cost of transport were both integral to the growth of trade. In the 1500s, the 'Columbian exchange' brought corn, potatoes and chillies from the Americas to Europe, and oranges, sugar and pigs to the Americas. Tragically, it also brought diseases such as smallpox, measles, influenza and chickenpox to the Americas, killing more than four-fifths of the population in some places.

Another abominable aspect of trade was the trafficking of more than 12 million people across the Atlantic Ocean between 1501 and 1866.[1] The scale of this brutal enterprise is mind-boggling.[2] In the 1700s, Europeans trafficked around 10 per cent of Africa's population across the Atlantic. Packed onto ships, underfed and vulnerable to disease, over one in ten captured people did not survive the journey. In slave markets, it was routine to separate parents from their children, and spouses from one another. An analysis of the New Orleans slave market (the largest in the United States) estimates that more than four-fifths of people sold were separated from immediate family members.[3]

The Portuguese were responsible for almost half of all enslaved people taken, with Brazil being the destination for more than one-third of them. The Spanish, French and Dutch were also prominent slave traders. In destination colonies in the Caribbean and the Americas, enslaved people were forced to work on labour-intensive crops – initially sugar, then cotton and tobacco. Slave holding was a major source of wealth in some European nations, accounting for around 5 per cent of British national income by the late 1700s and helping fuel that country's industrial development.[4]

During the same era, gold and silver became vital exports. From 1500 to 1800, tens of thousands of tonnes of silver were shipped to Spain from Mexico and Bolivia. However, in an era of hostility between European powers, sailors could not expect safe passage if they encountered ships from other nations. In one incident, English explorer-turned-pirate Francis Drake robbed a Spanish ship carrying 36 kilograms (79 pounds) of gold and 26 tonnes (29 US tons) of silver. He was lauded as a hero in England and reviled as a criminal in Spain.

But perhaps Spain should not have been so outraged by Drake's theft, because the massive influx of gold and silver would ultimately harm its economy.[5] Precious metals were the currency of the day, so the arrival of ships laden with gold and silver was the equivalent of a modern government printing too much money. Prices of goods and services rose. Imports grew and exports shrank. Tellingly, the region where the precious metals arrived, Andalusia, suffered earliest. Spanish manufacturers of ships, rope and silk found themselves unable to compete on the world market, and their businesses collapsed. In 1500, Spain was one of the world's wealthiest nations. Two centuries later, it was a backwater. An echo of Spain's experience is the modern-day resource curse, in which valuable mineral assets can end up impoverishing a nation. Among low-income nations, those with significant resource deposits tend to grow more slowly.

THE MEDICI

Among the most successful philanthropists in history were Italy's Medici family. By sponsoring a slew of artists, including Brunelleschi, Botticelli, Da Vinci, Michelangelo and Raphael, they helped bring about the Italian Renaissance. They supported astronomer Galileo Galilei, commissioned Florence's Boboli Gardens and built the Uffizi Gallery.

Originally from a village in northern Tuscany, members of the Medici family moved to Florence in the twelfth century, making their living in the textile trade. In 1397, the family formed the Medici Bank, which became the largest bank in Europe. They were among the first to use double-entry book-keeping, and benefited from Florence's strength in crafts, controlled by a series of powerful guilds.

As bankers, the Medici family had an interest in economic stability, and formed relationships with other powerful families in Florence. Their focus was on acquiring resources through trade, not seizing land through military conquest. For most of the 1400s, Florence was ruled by three generations of the Medici: Cosimo, Piero and Lorenzo.

Lorenzo de' Medici, dubbed Lorenzo the Magnificent, was the most significant patron of the Italian Renaissance.

The rule of the Medici in Florence was interrupted on two occasions (1494–1512 and 1527–1530), but they continued to build their power across Italy. Between 1513 and 1605, the Medici family produced four popes of the Catholic Church – Pope Leo X, Pope Clement VII, Pope Pius IV and Pope Leo XI. In the same era, the family also produced two queens of France: Catherine de' Medici and Marie de' Medici. The family's power waned in the eighteenth century, but their enduring impact on art and architecture continues to inspire wealthy patrons today.

Although European colonialists brought deadly viruses, they were also susceptible to local diseases. Because the risks varied dramatically, disease patterns shaped the patterns of colonialism in the 'Age of Discovery'.[6] In the early 1600s, the English Pilgrim Fathers considered sailing the *Mayflower* to Guyana in South America, but ultimately chose the United States because of the high mortality rates in Guyana. In West Africa, malaria and other tropical diseases claimed the lives of about half of all European settlers in the first year after arriving – effectively thwarting attempts to establish roads and institutions. There was little incentive to invest in areas where the chance of dying was so terrifyingly high.

In countries where settler mortality was relatively low, such as Canada, the United States, Chile and Australia, colonial powers invested in everything from railways to universities. In nations where settler mortality was high – such as Nigeria, Angola and Madagascar – the relationship was fundamentally extractive, designed to remove as much wealth as possible. Settlers took slaves, gold and other precious commodities. The extractive approach reached its nadir at the end of the colonial era, when Belgium's King Leopold II ruthlessly exploited the Congo: killing, maiming and stealing from the native population. Though nothing can excuse the barbarism of extractive colonialism, the differing prevalence of malaria helps explain why European settlers invested far more in the United States than in West Africa, and why the trans-Atlantic slave trade went from east to west, rather than the other way around.

Colonialism was not always a government enterprise. The

largest company in history may well have been the Dutch East India Company, a multinational formed in 1602 by the merger of several trading companies. Over the next two centuries, the Dutch East India Company maintained armed forces, built forts, concluded treaties with native rulers and generally behaved like a colonial power. It traded in spices, silk, coffee, sugarcane and wine, owned hundreds of ships and employed tens of thousands of people. With its operations centred on Indonesia, the company had major outposts in China, Japan, India, Sri Lanka and South Africa.

Because investors could buy shares in the Dutch East India Company, it was the world's first public company. From the standpoint of investors, this was attractive because it pooled risk. Rather than chancing everything on a single ship, shareholders could invest a small amount in many different shipping expeditions. Seafaring was potentially profitable but also immensely hazardous. Pirates, storms and scurvy could doom a voyage. Prices might suddenly change. Just as most modern investors prefer a broad portfolio of stocks, the investors of the 1600s preferred to put their money in a big company. Investors also liked the fact that the Dutch East India Company was a monopoly, with the Dutch government granting it an exclusive power to operate in Asia on behalf of the Netherlands. But consumers paid the price, as the company used its market position to overcharge on routes that it controlled.

Much the same was true of the British East India Company, whose monopoly allowed it to mint money, raise an army, collect taxes, run criminal trials and transport enslaved people from Asia and Africa. In the Indonesian Maluku Islands, then known as the Spice Islands, conflict between the company and its Dutch counterpart helped provoke four Anglo-Dutch wars. In India, the power of the British East India Company was largely unchecked. Through force of arms and treaties with Indian provincial rulers, the British East India Company came to control two-thirds of the Indian subcontinent – the area that makes up modern-day India, Pakistan and Bangladesh.[7] The British East India company has touched our world in astonishing ways. Its tea was dumped into Boston Harbor at the start of the American Revolution, and conflict over its opium sales to China sparked the Opium Wars. Tea merchant Thomas Twining and university benefactor Elihu Yale got their start working for the British East India Company (the company fired Yale for corruption, and his ill-gotten gains helped kickstart the university that bears his name).

A print depicting ships of the British East India Company leaving Woolwich.

Risk on the high seas called forth ingenious economic solutions. In Ancient Greece, those organising a shipping voyage sold 'bottomry bonds', which paid a high rate of interest if the ship reached port, but nothing if it sank. In 1293, Portugal's King Denis established Europe's first marine insurance fund, allowing merchants to organise voyages without bearing the entire risk of catastrophe.[8] The origins of insurance remain relevant today. Insurance is most useful when it covers a ruinous risk: the house burning down, crashing into an expensive car, the death of a family's sole earner. But if the cost of an item is less than a month's income, you're probably better taking the risk. Insure your home, not your mobile phone.

Throughout history, one of the greatest risks humans have faced is running out of resources. And if you don't have much money to begin with, poverty is hard to insure against. In the Middle Ages, before social insurance, the destitute received little help. In England, assistance for those who were unable to work emerged from a strong moral sense that welfare was only for the 'deserving poor'. In the 1500s, begging was punished by whipping, jail, branding (with the letter 'V' for vagabond) and even hanging. This left many who were unable to work with a choice between starvation or punishment.

In France, the Moulins Ordinance of 1561 established a system of poor relief that required local authorities to provide assistance to the poor, while empowering authorities to demand that able-bodied individuals work in exchange for any aid they received. A similar philosophy underpinned the English Poor Laws of 1601, which provided meagre rations through parishes, but withheld these 'parish loaves' from the 'undeserving poor'. Even when society could afford to feed those who were starving, there was an excessive concern that providing aid could blunt the incentive to work.

Shakespeare wrote most of his plays between 1590 and 1610. Watching *Hamlet* or *Romeo and Juliet*, the Bard and his generation can feel close to us, grappling with the same challenges of love, hope and betrayal. There are even economic lessons – *The Tempest* reminds us of the hazards of global commerce, *The Merchant of Venice* explores the problem of enforcing contracts and *Henry IV* contains insightful observations on scarcity.

But in another sense, the world of Shakespeare was a long way away. His was an age of slavery and superstition. During the 1500s and 1600s, nearly one million people were killed for the crime of witchcraft. Such was the scale of the brutality that in one German town, 400 were killed on a single day. Most of the victims were poor women, many of them widows. In one intriguing analysis, economist Emily Oster shows that bad harvests were a strong predictor of witchcraft trials.[9] When economic conditions deteriorated, people looked for a scapegoat. The most active period of witchcraft trials coincided with the coldest periods of the 'little ice age': in the 1590s and between 1680 and 1730.

TULIP MANIA

Tulips were introduced to Europe from the Ottoman Empire in the mid-1500s. Their intense colours made them unlike any flower seen in Europe at the time. Botanists bred different varieties, creating a profusion of colours. Horticulturalists discovered that by infecting the bulbs with the mosaic virus, it was possible to create petals streaked with a second colour.

With their strong financial markets, the Netherlands became the epicentre for tulips during the 1600s. Tulip sales occurred in the dormant phase, from June to September, when bulbs can be dug up and relocated.

As tulip mania grew, the prices of tulips infected with the mosaic virus surged. This was not entirely irrational, since a fashionable tulip could only be propagated by budding the infected mother bulb, not through ordinary seed propagation. In 1625, a Semper Augustus tulip bulb sold for 2000 guilders, the modern equivalent of US$16,000.[10] In 1637, prices crashed.

The Semper Augustus tulip caused a stir in 1620s Europe.

The collapse of the tulip market is often referred to as one of history's first financial bubbles. But like all good tales, this one contains elements of exaggeration. Economists observe that the extraordinary prices were only paid for the scarcest bulbs (those infected with mosaic virus), and that prices fell by around two-thirds to four-fifths over a five-year period – not as dramatic a drop as has sometimes been reported.

Tulip mania encouraged the flowering of innovation. By the early 1700s, Dutch botanists had created many new varieties, and the hyacinth replaced the tulip as Europe's most fashionable flower. Unlike other financial bubbles, tulip mania did not affect the Dutch economy, which continued to prosper throughout this era.

4

THE INDUSTRIAL REVOLUTION AND THE WEALTH OF NATIONS

IN THE SWEEP OF HUMAN history, rising living standards are a relatively new phenomenon. As we have seen, the agricultural revolution enabled populations to expand, but the material circumstances for most people barely changed. In Japan, the average real income was US$2.80 a day in 1000, and US$2.90 a day in 1700.[1] This was not an exceptional story: it would have been unusual in this era for children to live more prosperous lives than their parents. Indeed, one economic historian goes further, arguing that in the 1700s most of the world's population lived lives that were no better than their ancestors' on the African savannah.[2] They were no taller, their life expectancy was no longer, and they consumed no more calories. The tea-sippers who populate Jane Austen's novels were the rare exception in a world where poverty was the norm. Mostly, economic growth had led to a bigger population, not a better standard of living.

All that changed with the industrial revolution. Since then, life expectancy at birth has doubled, real incomes have increased fourteen-fold, and average heights have increased by around 10 centimetres (4 inches).[3] In the modern economy, we expect growth to deliver higher living standards with each successive generation. But before the industrial revolution, economic growth was patchy and slow.

Economist Robert Allen argues that the best way of understanding the industrial revolution is as a set of interlocking revolutions.[4] English agriculture was highly productive, thanks to selective plant breeding, improved soil tillage, and rotation of crops. Because fewer people were required to produce food, England experienced an 'urban revolution', with one-quarter of the population living in cities by 1750. Urbanisation, in turn, fuelled a 'commercial revolution': a product of the dense social networks in London and other English cities. Imports and exports grew rapidly, and private banks emerged to facilitate the shipping trade. Cities also enabled innovation. As economist Alfred Marshall would later note, physical proximity creates something 'in the air' – an environment in which new ideas are rapidly shared and improved. Just as technology firms today are more productive in Silicon Valley, industrialists were more productive in the English cities of the industrial revolution.

Among the interlocking revolutions, the most important was technological. During the 1700s, 'a wave of gadgets swept over England'.[5] James Hargreaves's spinning jenny let workers spin multiple threads, eventually making the process of producing cotton thread 100 times more efficient in a single generation.[6] The iron industry was transformed by using coke rather than charcoal, the puddling process to produce bar iron, and larger blast furnaces. Thomas Newcomen invented the steam engine in 1712, and James Watt refined it in the 1760s and 1770s. England's abundant coal reserves were important to the success of steam and began contributing to the build-up of atmospheric carbon that we now know causes climate change.

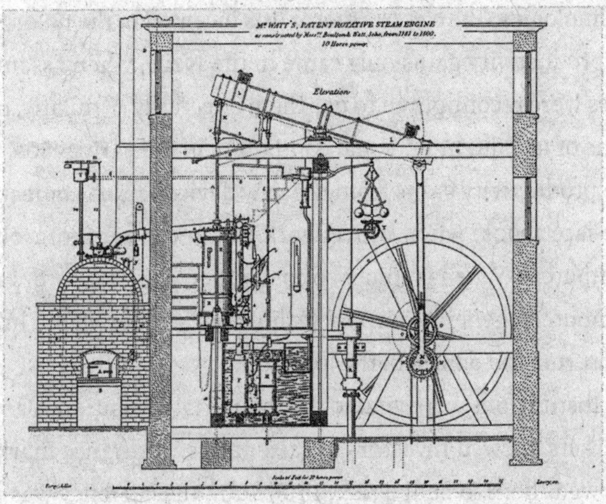

James Watt's coal-powered steam engine, patented in 1769.

'General-purpose technologies' are innovations that can supercharge economic development, but often take time to have an impact. Coal-powered steam engines ultimately revolutionised factories, transformed shipping and enabled train travel. Yet it took time for manufacturers to make the most of coal power. When James Watt's patent expired in 1800, British factories were still using three times as much water power as coal power.[7] The first major railway line – from Liverpool to Manchester – did not open until 1830. It was not until the middle of the century that half the growth in Britain's labour productivity was due to coal. One reason the industrial revolution lasted such a long time is that it took almost a century for people to properly harness coal.

The same pattern can be seen with other general-purpose technologies. The electric motor was invented in the 1880s, but its productivity gains only came in the 1920s, when assembly lines were reconfigured to use them effectively. Similarly, millions of us bought personal computers in the early 1980s, but the productivity gains from the new devices didn't come until the late 1990s, when office work was reconfigured around computers. When it comes to coal power, electric motors and computers, general-purpose technologies underwhelm in the short run and dazzle in the long run.

Institutions were vital to the industrial revolution. Capital markets allowed investors to raise funds. Insurance markets allowed them to hedge risk. In Britain, the currency was relatively stable and law courts were relatively independent. The power of the British monarchy was constrained, and its parliamentarians were generally well disposed towards industry and entrepreneurship. This created a fertile environment for risk-taking and long-term investment.[8]

Modern economics emerged from the same crucible as the industrial revolution. On 8 March 1776, James Watt's first profitable dual-cylinder steam engine entered the market.[9]

The next day another Scotsman, Adam Smith, published *The Wealth of Nations*, a foundational economics text. *The Wealth of Nations* was the product of a startlingly original mind. Smith went to the University of Glasgow at age fourteen, then began his postgraduate work at Oxford's Balliol College, starting at age seventeen. Smith's nonconformist thinking may have been shaped by his Oxford experience. As one biographer wrote, his college was 'Jacobite, Tory, factional, costly and Scotophobic; and Adam Smith was Presbyterian, Whiggish, sociable, impecunious and a Scot'.[10] Smith was passionate and eccentric. He is said to have once walked out of his house in his dressing gown, thinking about economics, and only realised his error when he reached the next town, 19 kilometres (12 miles) away. On another occasion, he apparently fell into a tanning pit while animatedly discussing free trade.[11]

The Wealth of Nations begins with a description of a pin factory. Working alone, Smith argued, a worker would be lucky to make one pin a day. But a team of ten people, specialising in different parts of pin-making, could produce 4,800 pins per person per day. He also showed how people's apparent self-interest can be socially beneficial in a market system, noting that, 'It is not from the benevolence of the butcher, the brewer, or the baker, that we expect our dinner, but from their regard to their own interest.' Markets play a powerful coordinating role. That's why you're more likely to see shortages of meat, beer and bread in a command economy than a capitalist economy.

Smith didn't think that markets were perfect. Unlike some of the economists who would follow him, he was worried about monopolies, the excessive influence of business on politics, and collusion between companies. 'People of the same trade seldom meet together,' he wrote 'but the conversation ends in a conspiracy against the public, or in some contrivance to raise prices.' At the time, there was little to prevent companies colluding against the public interest, exploiting their market power to raise prices well above the cost of production, and co-opting government into passing laws that deterred new entrants.

Just as the industrial revolution was beginning, political revolutions were occurring on both sides of the Atlantic. The American Declaration of Independence (1776) and the French Revolution (beginning in 1789) had their origins in the principle of individual liberty. Just as markets aggregate individual preferences into prices and quantities, democratic elections aggregate individual preferences to choose governments. More than two centuries on, the evidence is clear: living standards are higher in market economies than controlled economies. Likewise, democracies tend to be richer, and spend more on health and education. Never in history have two fully democratic countries gone to war.[12]

Free markets and democracy don't always go together, but there's a certain synergy between them. The collapse of feudalism showed people that they could choose their own careers. As they gained more economic independence, it was natural that people also wanted a say in choosing their own governments.

Yet these were also war-ravaged times. For two decades, from 1792 to 1815, the French waged a series of conflicts –

known as the Revolutionary and Napoleonic Wars – against a rolling series of European adversaries. By the time of Napoleon's final defeat in 1815, millions of men had been killed. Such expensive conflicts also had macroeconomic consequences. Like many governments since, the British government in the 1790s decided to pay for its armaments by printing more banknotes. Since 1717, Britain had operated under a gold standard, which allowed holders of banknotes to exchange them for gold. Having massively increased the money supply, the British government temporarily suspended the right of banknote holders to exchange them for gold and increased the price level by 59 per cent over three years. A disparaging cartoon led critics to call the Bank of England 'the Old Lady', a name that persists today.[13] The

James Gillray's cartoon satirising the government's financial policy led people to call the Bank of England 'the Old Lady'.

gold standard would be largely abandoned during the Great Depression, partially reinstated in the 1944 Bretton Woods Agreement, and permanently dumped in the early 1970s.

Economic thinking of this time had its roots in philosophy. 'It is the greatest happiness of the greatest number', wrote philosopher Jeremy Bentham in 1776, 'that is the measure of right and wrong'. Bentham is generally regarded as the founder of modern utilitarianism – the notion that if we have a choice, we should prefer the outcome that produces the greatest good for the greatest number of people.

Utilitarianism can seem obvious at times. If a ship is sinking, and you can safely fit twice as many people on the lifeboats, then the outcome is twice as good. But utilitarianism can also produce uncomfortable conclusions. With a train bearing down upon five people, would you flick a switch to send it on a track where it would kill one person instead? If you were in a medical centre, with five people about to die because they needed a different organ, would you harvest the necessary body parts from the next healthy person to walk in the door?

Despite its occasionally discomforting implications, utilitarianism is the main framework of thinking that economists use today. Building on the work of Bentham, English economist William Stanley Jevons brought an increasingly mathematical approach, explaining the notion of diminishing marginal utility. Anyone who's enjoyed the first glass of water on a hot day more than the second glass has experienced diminishing marginal utility. This simple principle has surprisingly wide implications. It explains why most people prefer a varied diet and enjoy travelling to different places. Across people, diminishing marginal utility can be used to make the case for progressive taxes and social welfare. If a dollar brings more happiness to a battler than a billionaire, then redistribution can improve overall utility. The battler might use the money to visit a dentist, while the billionaire might choose slightly better upholstery on their private jet.

English philosopher John Stuart Mill shaped the notion of *Homo economicus*: modelling people as seeking to maximise wellbeing.[14] Mill also helped introduce the notion of opportunity cost – the value of the next best thing that you give up. For example, working an overnight shift has a higher opportunity cost than working a day shift. Overnights mean missing out on a regular night's sleep and time socialising with friends and family. Likewise, taking time off work to study a full-time Master of Business Administration comes at the opportunity cost of lost earnings. Opportunity cost can also be a helpful way of making decisions. For example, if you're undecided about an expensive purchase, a handy rule of thumb is to compare it with the next best way you might spend that amount of money. Perhaps the opportunity cost of buying that stylish outfit is not seeing your favourite band in concert.

Intellectual developments of the time were shaped by the inventions of the age. In 1835, German chemist Justus von Liebig invented the modern mirror, by depositing a thin layer of silver onto glass. For the first time in history, people could accurately see what they looked like. As historian Steven Johnson notes, 'Before mirrors came along, the average person went through life without ever seeing a truly accurate representation of his or her face, just fragmentary, distorted glances in pools of water or polished metals.'[15] Mirrors enabled artists to paint self-portraits. They created a more self-centred world, which helped fuel modern capitalism and the market system. In turn, this led to more sales of mirrors.

Clocks also reshaped society. With the invention of the pendulum, clocks became more accurate than sundials, and household clocks began to proliferate. Watches became considerably more accurate with the invention of the balance spring. Inventors added a minute hand (which previously wasn't sufficiently accurate to bother with) as the precision of their timekeeping devices improved. This allowed factories to set shift schedules with a reasonable expectation that workers would show up on time. It facilitated train travel, which relied on timetables. Accurate timekeeping was also a boon to sea travel, since ocean chronometers made it possible to determine a ship's longitude. Quality clocks accelerated the transition from cottage production to mass production, from home schooling to public schooling, and from the irregular rhythms of the pre-industrial era to the discipline of the industrial age.[16]

Not everyone was excited by the new inventions that underpinned the industrial revolution. In 1811, a group of aggrieved textile workers met in secret and wrote to factory owners under the pen name 'Ned Ludd', threatening to smash mechanical knitting machines if they continued to be used. Thousands joined their cause. Legend had it that Ned Ludd lived in Sherwood Forest, like Robin Hood. The Luddites even received support from poet Lord Byron, who used his first speech to the House of Lords to argue that the Luddites were 'honest and industrious', and that their violence was a product of 'the most unparalleled distress'. His was a minority view. The British government passed laws making machine-breaking a capital offence, and mobilised so many soldiers against them that at one point there were more troops fighting the Luddites than battling Napoleon. Hundreds of Luddites were transported to Australia for their crimes.

An engraving depicting Ned Ludd, the fictional figurehead for the Luddite movement.

While the real wages of handloom weavers fell during this period, the Luddites were wrong to claim that technological changes would cause mass unemployment.[17] In the decade from 1811 to 1821, the number of jobs in the British economy increased by more than 10 per cent.[18]

Britain's parish-based welfare system assumed that those distributing welfare knew the recipients personally, which became increasingly difficult as the population grew and mobility increased. This led to the creation of impersonal workhouses, a system that assumed the poor were inherently lazy, and therefore should only be given sustenance in exchange for hard work. Britain's new Poor Law, enacted in 1834, used workhouses to provide food and housing to those in need.

Women at the Westminster Union workhouse.

But workhouses did not want to feed everyone, so they added features that made things especially unpleasant for residents, such as prison-like uniforms, and the separation of men and women. Given that Britain's elite were the 'landed gentry', who made their money from inherited real estate, it seems likely that the poor worked a good deal harder than the rich. The hypocrisy was not lost on nineteenth-century novelists such as George Eliot, Thomas Hardy and Charles Dickens, who chronicled the brutality of the workhouse system. In Ireland, the country's poor law proved utterly inadequate when the potato crop failed in the 1840s. Around one million people died, and a similar number fled the country.

Forced to compete against new products, industrialists often turned to governments for help. These claims were mocked by French economist Frédéric Bastiat, who wrote a satirical petition arguing that candlestick makers could not possibly compete against 'the ruinous competition of a rival who apparently works under conditions so far superior to our own for the production of light'. In order to compete against this rival – the sun – the petition asked for a law requiring that curtains be closed at all times. Doing so, it argued, would create jobs for farmers, whalers and candelabra manufacturers.

Writing tongue-in-cheek, Bastiat was making a key economic point: the costs of blocking new technologies are often unseen. If people use more candles, they will have to cut back their spending in other areas. In another faux petition, Bastiat implored the government to ban everyone from using their right hand, on the basis that this would vastly increase the demand for workers. This is sometimes known as the 'lump of labour' fallacy – the idea that there is a fixed amount of work to be done, which can be simply reallocated across the population. In fact, because workers are also consumers, changes that make employees less productive are likely to reduce their earnings, which will shrink their spending, which will in turn have a negative impact on the economy.

Bastiat has been dubbed 'the most brilliant economic journalist who ever lived'.[19] His impact on economics is all the more remarkable given that Bastiat's public career lasted just six years, before his life was cut short by tuberculosis. Although the principles of economics were mostly shaped by British and North American thinkers, French thinkers were especially influential in the 1700s and 1800s. The terms 'entrepreneur' and 'laissez faire' (let it be) reflect this period of French influence.

The technological changes of the industrial revolution were paralleled by the growth of trade. By the 1800s, trade had transformed the lives of people around the world. Cotton and woollen products flooded into China, along with matches, needles, umbrellas and window glass.[20] The average European drank tea, consumed chocolate and traded with silver coins.

Not everyone liked trade, for the simple reason that a cheaper import can drive domestic producers out of business. Recognising this, producers may lobby for laws to block imports. A few who will lose a lot tend to be more politically influential than many who will gain a little. This remains true even if the total gains of the many outweigh the losses of the few. This political dynamic led Britain in 1815 to impose a tariff on grain imports to protect local farmers, with the result that British wheat cost twice as much as Dutch wheat.[21] The fight over the Corn Laws would prove to be a pivotal point in the development of economics. One of the early campaigners against the tariffs was David Ricardo.

At a young age, Ricardo made a large fortune as a stockbroker. He then turned to politics and intellectual life, buying a seat in parliament. He became fascinated by economics, discovering Adam Smith's work while on holiday, and deciding to devote his parliamentary career to abolishing the Corn Laws, which Ricardo believed would make Britain 'the happiest country in the world'.[22] Ricardo's writings are harder to follow than Smith's, with a fellow member of parliament describing Ricardo as one who 'argued as if he had dropped from another planet'.[23] Yet he introduced the idea of comparative advantage (which we saw earlier) – a principle that is fundamental to explaining why even the most unproductive nation can benefit from trade. Although Ricardo died before the Corn Laws were scrapped, he played a vital role in putting Britain on the path towards free trade.

5

TRADE, TRAVEL AND TECHNOLOGY TAKE OFF

IN THE 1840S, A SERIES of failed harvests pushed up British grain prices. The decade came to be known as the 'hungry forties'. The growing power of urban industrialists added to the pressure on rural aristocrats. For a while, economics held centre stage in English political debate. In 1843, *The Economist* was founded with the help of the Anti-Corn Law League. In the words of Walter Bagehot, an early editor of the magazine, 'There has never, perhaps, been another time in the history of the world when excited masses of men and women hung on the words of one talking political economy.'[1] The debate over free trade roiled the nation, and was commemorated in poems, needlework, busts and cakes.[2] In 1846, the Corn Laws were abolished. According to one analysis, only the top 10 per cent of Britons were left worse off, with the bottom 90 per cent benefiting. The forces of free trade had won the battle.

Elsewhere, trade was a literal battle. In response to the Chinese government's refusal to allow British traders to import opium, British warships attacked on behalf of the drug dealers. In a series of battles around Guangzhou, Hong Kong, Hangzhou, Ningbo and Zhenjiang, more than 3,000 people were killed. One scholar calls Britain's attacks a case of 'narco-imperialism'.[3] The conflict led to the 1842 Treaty of Nanking, under which China agreed to open five additional ports to trade and to hand over the territory of Hong Kong to the British. Within four decades, opium imports to China topped 6,000 tonnes a year.[4]

A depiction of the Battle of Chinkiang (now Zhenjiang) in July 1842.

Buoyed by the success of Britain's 'trade or die' policies, the United States sent four warships to Japan in 1853, demanding the country end restrictions on trade. The invasion helped end Japan's shogun era, a seven-century period in which the country was led by military dictators. The last shoguns, the Tokugawa shogunate, curtailed trade, limited diplomatic ties and banned virtually all travel into or out of Japan. The 1867 Meiji restoration, which consolidated power in the hands of the emperor of Japan, began opening Japan to the world. The Meiji government also had a strong emphasis on education, which in turn allowed the country to adopt technology more rapidly.

Under the slogan 'rich country, strong army', Japan's modernisers abolished the caste system and allowed people to take any job.[5] Samurai warriors – then numbering nearly two million – were replaced by a national army and compulsory military service for all men. Japan's government prioritised investments in railway and telegraph systems, and adapted Western technologies to account for the fact that labour was cheaper in Japan than it was in Europe and North America. A treaty with Western powers had capped Japanese tariffs at 5 per cent, so the country could not keep out foreign competition. Instead, state-led economic development became vital to the country's rapid productivity improvements.

American polymath Benjamin Franklin once wrote that 'no nation was ever ruined by trade'. Yet even as they were encouraging other countries to open up, Europe and North America were imposing tariffs on imports. This was partly due to the need for revenue. Before broad-based income taxes, tariffs were a major source of revenue for many nations. Wars such as the Napoleonic Wars and the US Civil War were often funded by an increase in tariffs.

Tariffs were easy to administer and good for the government budget, but bad for the economy as a whole. Tariffs have been likened to a country impeding shipping by putting rocks in its own harbours. Removing the rocks (abolishing tariffs) benefits a country regardless of what its trading partners do. But in practice, countries have often put more political weight on exports than imports. Under this 'mercantilist' approach, nations agree to cut tariffs only if their trading partner does the same. An early deal of this type came in 1860, when Britain agreed to remove almost all tariffs in exchange for France reducing its tariffs. The agreement included a 'most favoured nation' clause, which means that the trading partner also gets the best deal offered to any other nation. Over the next decade or so, trade agreements were struck across Europe, and their most favoured nation clauses helped spread free trade across the continent.[6] Trade had the effect of 'unbundling' production and consumption.[7] Trade means that things no longer need to be made and sold in the same country.

Trade in this period ought to have helped the poorest nations grow. After all, empires typically operated as free trade areas. The opening of the Suez Canal in 1869 almost halved the seagoing distance from London to the Arabian Sea. But imperial powers tightly constrained the range of goods exported from their colonies, and managed trade for the benefit of the centre over the periphery. During this era, the economies of Western Europe began to pull away from the rest of the world. From 1820 to 1900, living standards in Europe more than doubled, while living standards in Asia and Africa did not rise at all.[8]

The idea of the corporation was fundamental to advancing the industrial revolution. Just as the Dutch and British

East India Companies allowed investors to pool risks across multiple seafaring expeditions, so too industrial corporations let financiers share the risk of new ventures in this era. Companies had existed since Roman times, but they proved vital in the case of risky ventures, such as exploring for mineral deposits, building railways into new regions, or selling an exotic product. Corporations also encouraged specialisation, by providing a vehicle through which a rich investor might back the business idea of a penniless entrepreneur. In 1855, the United Kingdom passed the *Limited Liability Act*, which provided that if a company collapsed, creditors could not recover their debts by pursuing the shareholders personally.

Corporations solved the problem of how to get investors to put money into risky ventures: limit the downside so that owners cannot lose more than they invest. But corporations also became large employers, whose bargaining power massively exceeded that of their individual workers. The solution to this problem was the creation of the trade union, in which workers organised to demand better pay and conditions. However, during the early decades of the industrial revolution, unions were illegal. In 1834, six English agricultural workers, who came to be known as the Tolpuddle Martyrs, were transported to Australia as punishment for forming a union. After public marches and a petition signed by 800,000 supporters, their sentences were overturned. It was a sign of the strong community support for workers' rights.

The gains from the industrial revolution took a surprisingly long time to flow to British workers. By the 1830s, half a century after the start of the industrial revolution, real wages had hardly grown. Other markers showed a similar pattern. British life expectancy in the early 1800s was between thirty-five and forty, barely higher than it had been in the 1500s.[9] Moreover, city-dwellers could expect to live a decade less than rural residents, as a lack of sanitation and cramped conditions contributed to the spread of disease. Medicine in this era did little to help: bloodletting with leeches, consuming mercury and taking shots of whisky were common treatments. But in the 1840s, British wages began to rise, along with other markers of development. From 1820 to 1870, the literacy rate increased from half to three-quarters of the population.[10]

Alongside the industrial revolution came industrial-scale warfare. From 1861 to 1865, the US Civil War ravaged the country. With the use of mass-produced weapons, railroads, steamships and telegraphs, the Civil War was industrial in its scale, and in its carnage. More than 600,000 combatants – one in five soldiers – lost their lives. At the end of the war, more than three million enslaved people were freed.

To economists, one of the striking features of the Civil War is the imbalance in resources between the two sides. A larger population and bigger economy do not guarantee victory (particularly if one side is willing to devote a greater share of its resources to the conflict). But money matters. As the saying goes, God is usually on the side of the bigger battalions.

At the outset of the war, the North had a population of 21 million, more than twice the South's population of 9 million.

The South was a primarily agricultural economy, with the North producing 90 per cent of the country's manufactured goods. Critically, the North produced 97 per cent of the country's firearms.

From an economic standpoint, the notable feature of the war is that the South held out as long as it did. Poor military tactics on the part of the North helped prolong the war, but ultimately the economic disparity between the two regions determined the outcome. During the course of the Civil War, the South funded 60 per cent of its costs through inflation (compared with 13 per cent for the north).[11] By the end of the war, the South was printing so much money that goods cost ninety-two times as much as they had done when the conflict began.

This was an era in which nations had been established, but travel across borders was essentially unimpeded. Few people held passports, and going to another country was simply a matter of boarding a train or ship. In 1851, massive gold discoveries in the Australian town of Ballarat caused an influx of migrants. Over the ensuing two decades, Australia's settler population quadrupled, from 440,000 to 1.7 million. A century earlier, the British colonialists had seen Australia as little more than an open-air prison. By the late-1800s, transportation of convicts had ceased, and migrants flowed in from Europe, Asia and the Americas. Many tried their luck at gold prospecting, but a substantial number worked in other industries, where wages were typically much higher than in the countries they were leaving.

OLD MASTERS AND YOUNG GENIUSES

Analysing creative careers, economist David Galenson has discovered an intriguing pattern.[12] Those who do their best work at a younger age tended to be conceptualists, driven by a single breakthrough idea. By contrast, those who produce their masterwork late in life are generally experimentalists, whose work is the gradual product of trial and error.

Among artists, Raphael, Johannes Vermeer, Vincent van Gogh and Pablo Picasso were conceptualists, who did their most important work early in their lives. Picasso painted his breakthrough cubist masterpiece *Les Demoiselles d'Avignon* at age twenty-five. Rembrandt, Michelangelo, Titian and Cézanne were experimentalists, who did their most important work late in life. Cézanne said he felt like he was always inching towards perfection.

The poets E. E. Cummings and Sylvia Plath found their inspiration internally and formulated their poems conceptually, producing their best work in their twenties and thirties. Meanwhile, Marianne Moore and Wallace Stevens drew on real experiences observed in their daily lives, producing their major works in their forties and beyond.

American poet Marianne Moore won the Pulitzer Prize and the National Book Award for her *Collected Poems* in 1951, aged sixty-three.

Conceptual novelists include James Joyce and Herman Melville, whose best work was created at a young age. Old masters include Charles Dickens and Virginia Woolf, whose experimentation sought to reflect the world around them. Movie director Orson Welles was a conceptual young genius, producing *Citizen Kane* at age twenty-six, while Clint Eastwood is an experimental old master, who only became an important director in his sixties.

Conceptualists find. Experimentalists seek.

Part of the reason that Australian workers earned more than their British and American counterparts was that employees were scarce. That gave Australian workers more power than northern hemisphere workers. After a strike in 1855, Sydney stonemasons were among the first workers in the world to win the right to an eight-hour day. With plenty of land and few people, Australian wages in the 1880s were the highest in the world, and the Australian labour movement came to play an influential role in politics. In the coming decades, Australia would be among the world's first countries to allow women to vote and stand for office, set a national minimum wage and hold elections on a Saturday (to maximise voter turnout).

Elsewhere, this era saw major developments in the welfare state. In the 1880s, with the social democrats gaining on him electorally, conservative German chancellor Otto von Bismarck introduced into parliament a package of reforms that provided health insurance, accident insurance and an old-age disability pension. The reforms were world-leading for the time, though modest by today's standards. The 'sickness funds' that underpinned Bismarck's health insurance programs were two-thirds funded by workers. Pensions were paid to those who passed the age of seventy, at a time when average thirty-year-old Germans could only expect to live to their early sixties.[13]

Meanwhile, some of the key innovations in health care came from France. By the 1860s, France had built one of the world's largest sewerage systems – mirroring the street layout. Writer Victor Hugo described it as 'a beautiful sewer;

the pure style reigns there'. In the mid-1800s, nations had begun to show off their new innovations at world fairs, and at France's 1867 International Exposition, visitors were offered tours of the sewer. Parisian homes were quickly connected to the new sewerage system, helping to reduce the prevalence of infectious diseases (we might call it 'the drain gain'). French scientist Louis Pasteur, who had lost three children to typhoid, developed the germ theory of disease and was instrumental in policies to provide cleaner drinking water and isolate infectious patients in hospitals. At the start of the industrial revolution, infectious diseases were a major reason why city-dwellers had higher mortality rates than their country cousins. Far-sighted governments made cities safer, which in turn spurred urbanisation.

Tourists visit Paris's state-of-the-art sewerage system designed by Eugène Belgrand and Baron Haussmann.

French obstetrician Stéphane Tarnier developed the humidicrib to sustain infants born prematurely. Visiting the Paris Zoo in 1880, Tarnier saw an exhibit of incubators for exotic birds and realised the same principle could be applied to newborn babies. Within three years, his invention had boosted the survival rate of underweight babies in his hospital from 35 per cent to 62 per cent.[14] Over the ensuing decades, better infant care would prove to be a key driver of rising life expectancy. Improvements in infant mortality saved many families the anguish of burying a child. And knowing their children were more likely to survive, women bore fewer babies. Reflecting the French focus on health reforms in this era, in 1893 the French government created a limited program of free health care for the destitute, which proved extremely popular, expanding in the following decade well beyond the expectations of those who designed the program.

Economic growth underpinned these social reforms, but it also allowed the concentration of economic power. In the United States, John D. Rockefeller's Standard Oil Company eliminated virtually all its competitors by buying them up or squeezing them out. By 1880, it controlled 90 per cent of the oil-refining business. Rockefeller and his associates then set up the Standard Oil Trust – a series of complex legal structures designed to shield the company's operations from scrutiny. Behind this shield, the organisation used its monopoly power to drive up prices and profits. In an attempt to tackle these problems, Congress passed the *Sherman Antitrust Act* in 1890. Yet it was not until the following decade that antitrust enforcement began in earnest – thanks partly to the work of investigative journalists such as Ida Tarbell, who uncovered the structures of the Standard Oil Company.

Not every attempt to put a spotlight on monopolies worked as intended. In the late-1800s, feminist writer Lizzie Magie was outraged by the power of 'robber barons' such as Cornelius Vanderbilt, John D. Rockefeller and Andrew Carnegie. Reading the ideas of economist Henry George introduced Magie to the way in which monopolies could allow extreme wealth and deep poverty to coexist. She subsequently developed a board game, dubbed 'The Landlord's Game', designed to serve as an interactive critique of monopoly power.

Wall Street was one of the most valuable streets on the board of the original Monopoly game, which was created as a radical warning.

Magie's motive was to show players how land grabbing enriched property owners and impoverished tenants. Yet when, three decades later, Parker Brothers produced a modified version of her game, stripped of its radical overtones and marketed to the public as 'Monopoly', the biggest monopolist became the winner. Magie was paid just US$500, but neither received the credit for her game nor achieved the lasting social justice impact she intended.

As the 1800s drew to a close, some of the world's fastest-growing cities were in the United States. One reason was that US city planners were more likely to lay out streets in a grid pattern, while many older European cities followed the local topography, or were laid out in a radial pattern. The radial layout made cities easier to defend, but grids are more economically efficient – maximising the use that can be made of street frontage, and making it easier to connect homes to sewerage and transport lines. Chicago is the world's most gridded city. Rome is one of the least gridded.[15]

Gridded cities tended to produce the world's first skyscrapers. By the 1890s, buildings of at least ten storeys could be found in Chicago, New York and St Louis. Two technologies were essential to skyscrapers. The Bessemer process enabled the mass production of steel beams that could hold the weight of the soaring structure. And the passenger elevator allowed people to reach the higher floors. While the technologies were available globally, regulation also influenced where they were constructed. Stricter fire safety and zoning laws constrained the development of skyscrapers in many

European cities during the early twentieth century, while US cities gave more freedom to developers. The differences can still be seen in the world's skylines.

6

ECONOMIC MODELS AND THE MODERN FACTORY

AT THE TURN OF THE twentieth century, Englishman Alfred Marshall was the world's most influential economist. His 1890 textbook *Principles of Economics* drew on his mathematical talents (he had achieved the prestigious rank of 'Second Wrangler' in his Cambridge maths exams) and was focused on how economics could improve social wellbeing. Supply and demand, Marshall wrote, were like the blades of a pair of scissors. In a graph with price on one axis and quantity on the other, the line representing supply generally slopes up because more people are willing to provide a good or service when the price is higher. The line representing demand tends to slope down because of the familiar concept of diminishing marginal utility: the more that consumers have of something, the less they are willing to pay for each additional unit. For suppliers, price and quantity increase together. For consumers, there is a negative relationship between price and quantity. In both cases, trade-offs are at play: higher prices cause new suppliers to stop making other things and focus on this one, while higher prices cause some existing buyers to stop consuming this thing in favour of its substitutes.

Where the two lines cross is the market equilibrium – the point at which supply meets demand. If Marshall had wanted to buy a diamond in 1900, he would have noted that the market reflected the willingness of buyers to acquire diamonds and sellers to part with them. The equilibrium price is the price at which the amount that sellers are willing to sell exactly matches the amount that buyers are willing to buy. Earlier economists had graphed supply and demand, but the chart is known as the 'Marshallian Cross' because his was the most complete and persuasive description of the model.[1]

Considering producers, Marshall distinguished between a company's fixed costs – such as the land and buildings it owns – and its variable costs – such as the labour and raw materials it uses. In the long run, a company will go out of business if it cannot cover the costs of maintaining and replacing its assets. But in the short term, what most affects the price that a company charges for its outputs are its variable costs. The price of cotton will be quickly affected by changes in the cost of water, while the impact of rising machinery costs will be felt more slowly.

Marshall was a skilled mathematician, but the popularity of his textbook was due to his ability to convey ideas through diagrams and examples – methods that economists have used to teach students ever since. As Marshall once summarised his system: '(1) Use mathematics as a shorthand language, rather than as an engine of inquiry. (2) Keep to them till you have done. (3) Translate into English. (4) Then illustrate by examples that are important in real life. (5) Burn the mathematics. (6) If you can't succeed in 4, burn 3. This last I did often.' In other words, economists should employ mathematics as a useful tool to illustrate the world – but not get carried away with esoteric mathematics that fails to shed light on how the economy works. More economists should follow Marshall's advice.

Marshall expressed important ideas with striking clarity. In some instances, it is surprising they came so late in history. Markets and mathematics had been around for thousands of years. 'Economics' comes from the Ancient Greek term *oikonomia*, which roughly translates as 'household management'. Ancient Greek mathematicians understood Pythagoras' theorem, could approximate pi, and knew how to estimate the area under a parabola. Yet a solid exposition of supply and demand only emerged around the turn of the twentieth century.

The early part of the twentieth century also saw the formation of a critical economic institution: the US Federal Reserve. The Fed was not the first central bank, but its quirky creation story bears retelling. In 1907, when a banking collapse threatened the system, leading financier J.P. Morgan had summoned colleagues to his Madison Avenue mansion and locked the door. 'This is the place to stop the trouble,' he told them. Morgan pledged millions of dollars to at-risk banks and persuaded his fellow bankers to do the same. The panic subsided.

Three years later, representatives of major US commercial banks again took the initiative, convening a secret ten-day meeting on Jekyll Island in Georgia. The bankers pretended they were on a duck-hunting trip, and boarded their train one at a time so as not to be seen together. One banker apparently even toted a shotgun to give the trip an air of authenticity. The report proposed the architecture of what would become the US Federal Reserve, eventually comprising twelve regional banks with the power to issue currency. Following some tense negotiations in Congress, the Federal Reserve was created in 1913. The United States would not be solely reliant on financial plutocrats to avert the next banking crisis.

Central banks had existed since the seventeenth century (the Bank of Amsterdam, the central bank of Stockholm and the Bank of England were all founded in the 1600s), but in the twentieth century, central banks increasingly took on the role of providing stability to the economic system. Regular commercial banks use money from short-term deposits to make long-term loans. Because they borrow short and lend long, even the best-managed bank is vulnerable to running out of cash if all its depositors simultaneously demand their money back. By guaranteeing people's deposits, a central bank can prevent bank runs, and make the financial system more stable. Typically, this doesn't involve a cent changing hands: once people know that their deposits are guaranteed, the panic is avoided. We might think of financial stability as a public good: a benefit that flows to everyone, undiminished by the number of people who enjoy a more stable system. In the modern era, central banks also have an important role in targeting inflation, to which we will return shortly.

The assembly line at Ford Motors, Dearborn, Michigan.

One of the hottest new products of the era was the automobile, and its evolution owes much to specialisation. At first, cars were as unaffordable as they were desirable, but in 1908 Peter Martin, an executive at Ford, proposed the idea of an assembly line. Martin got the idea from visiting a Chicago slaughterhouse, where carcasses moved between workers, who each sliced off a standard cut of meat. In a Detroit plant, experiments with assembly lines showed that they allowed workers to produce cars far more quickly. When the system was put into operation, vehicles came off the line so speedily that Ford decided it could no longer allow customers to choose the colour of their cars. It turned out that black paint dried fastest. Accordingly, Henry Ford decided that a customer 'can have a car painted any color that he wants so long as it is black'.[2] The assembly line is now a standard part of many manufacturing facilities, but at the time it was radical to flip the process: for the car to move towards the parts rather than the other way around.

Innovation reshaped retail too. In 1909, Harry Selfridge opened a new kind of department store in Oxford Street, London. Selfridges aimed to make shopping fun. He structured the store so that customers could handle items for sale, encouraged staff to make women shoppers feel welcome and trained them to specialise in different product lines. Selfridge cleverly positioned the perfume counter on the ground floor, invitingly called his customers 'guests', and ran ads with the line 'the customer is always right'.

Other retailers focused on price. In the United States, Frank Woolworth created a series of stores that sold products for five and ten cents. These 'five-and-dime stores' were said to operate on the principle 'pile 'em high and sell 'em cheap'.[3]

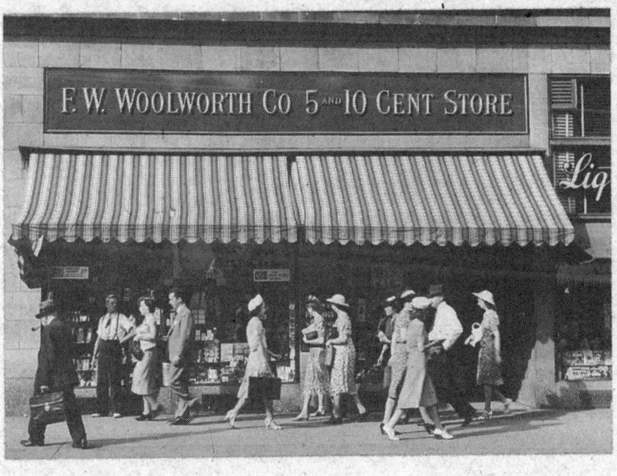

An early Woolworth store in New York.

In 1912, Woolworth floated on the stock market with 596 stores across the country. With such a large network of stores, they were able to use their buying power to negotiate lower prices with suppliers. Walmart, ÆON, Aldi, Tesco and Carrefour are modern heirs to this retail strategy, which delivers lower prices for consumers and fatter returns for shareholders, while squeezing suppliers and independent retailers.

Technological innovation shaped substance use too. In the 1880s, James Bonsack's cigarette-rolling machine had revolutionised the industry, and by the 1910s, cigarette consumption was rising rapidly (in the United States it would peak in the 1960s, with half of men smoking regularly). Heroin was marketed by Bayer from 1898 to 1910 as an over-the-counter cough suppressant. Cocaine was added to Coca-Cola until the early 1900s. In 1913, one expert claimed that nearly a quarter of US doctors were addicted to morphine.[4]

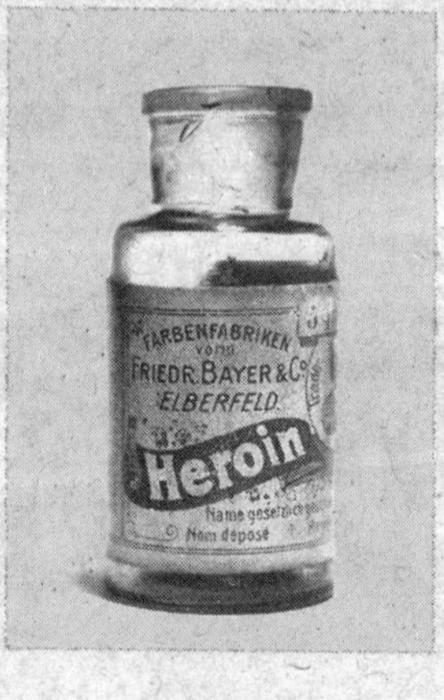

While effective, Bayer's cough medicine also proved highly addictive.

This was an era of mass migration. Passports were still rarely required. Just as migrants had flocked to the Australian gold fields, millions took advantage of the improvements in shipping technology to migrate from Russia to Canada, from Germany to New Zealand, or from the Netherlands to Indonesia. The new ships had steel hulls and were powered by coal engines. In the 1850s, it took migrants fifty-three days to sail from Liverpool to New York. By the 1910s, the journey had been cut to just eight days.[5] When economists look at migration, they mostly see people who are relocating to places where they feel safer, happier and more productive. Migrants are not just mouths to feed; they also bring muscles that build and minds that inspire. It is a mistake to see migrants as merely a new source of demand – they are also a new source of supply.

World War I broke this interconnected world. War came despite the strong commercial ties between the combatants (in 1914, Lloyd's of London insured most of the German shipping trade).[6] When the nations of Europe sleepwalked into war, much of the world's trade and migration ceased. And while its origins were unexpected, the ultimate result was not. At the outbreak of hostilities, the Allied powers (Britain, France, Russia and their allies) had far more resources than the Central powers (the German Empire, the Austro-Hungarian Empire and their allies). The Allied powers had five times the population, eleven times the territory and three times the income.[7]

The fact that the conflict took four years and claimed around 20 million lives reflects the ineptitude of the generals and the intransigence of the political leaders. But when the conflict ended, the side with the larger economic base had won.

In Russia, the turmoil was just beginning. The 1917 communist revolution promised 'peace, land and bread'. It delivered a six-year civil war and catastrophic economic outcomes. Average incomes quickly halved.[8] In some Russian cities, average caloric intake halved too. The conflict, the ensuing famine and the spread of infectious diseases led to 13 million premature deaths. Lenin's regime abolished private ownership of land and forbade the selling or renting of land. This prohibition would remain in place until 1990.

TRAGEDY OF THE COMMONS

Suppose that a group of farmers all have access to a common meadow, where they can let their cows graze. It would be in their collective interest to prevent overgrazing. But it is in each farmer's individual interest to put one more animal onto the commons. If the farmers fail to coordinate, then the likely outcome is that the pasture will be overgrazed.

The tragedy of the commons arises because each new cow imposes a small negative externality on the ecosystem. If the cow's owner does not pay anything for this externality, then the result can be a catastrophe. In the Newfoundland cod fishery off the coast of Canada, for example, the use of new fishing technology such as sonar led to a collapse in fish stocks, with the cod population falling to 1 percent of its historic level between 1985 and 1995.[9]

Elinor Ostrom analysed how some traditional groups developed rules to share common resources.

In other instances, communities have found ingenious solutions. In 2009, Elinor Ostrom became the first woman to win the Nobel Prize in Economics for her work on how local communities had managed common pool resources. In Nepal, rice farmers worked together to manage water. In Kenya, communities cooperated to manage forest resources. In Indonesia, local fishers carefully managed fish stocks.

The lesson of Ostrom's research is not that user management will always work, but that it is possible. In the successful cases, she observed, locals were actively involved in creating the rules, rather than having them imposed by outsiders. User management worked when enforcement was done by locals, with straightforward mechanisms for resolving disputes, and modest sanctions for initial breaches. The tragedy of the commons is not inevitable.

7

WORLD WAR I AND THE DEPRESSION

THE ECONOMIC DAMAGE OF WORLD War I went well beyond 1918. In the peace settlement, Germany was required to pay reparations of 132 billion gold marks (the sum was expressed in gold reserves). This was equivalent to around half of the country's pre-war wealth.[1] It was a vast amount; beyond anything the German economy could support, and the country's government struggled to make even the initial payments.[2]

To meet its debts, the German government began printing money. Lots of money. The resulting inflation steadily eroded the value of the German mark. Citizens sometimes needed wheelbarrows to carry their wages. The government produced new banknotes – first representing thousands of marks, then millions, then billions, then trillions. An item that cost 1 German mark in 1918 cost 1 trillion marks in 1923.

Hyperinflation creates havoc in the economy. Shoppers purchase everything on instalment, buying everything with part payments because unspent cash is losing value.

Restaurants must keep rewriting their menus. Taxis have to continually change their meters. On a single day in November 1923, the price of bread in Germany was seven times higher at the end of the day than it had been at the beginning.[3] Eventually, German policymakers restored the link between currency value and gold, bringing hyperinflation under control, and allowing Germany to enjoy a period of relative prosperity in the late 1920s. But memories of hyperinflation made policymakers excessively cautious in the face of the depression that was to come. Amid this economic turmoil, Hitler became chancellor in 1933.

Children play with almost worthless banknotes in the inflation-afflicted Weimer Republic.

The 'roaring twenties' saw the evolution of jazz, dancing and Art Deco. Across much of the advanced world, consumer spending and economic growth boomed. At a dinner on 15 October 1929, prominent Yale economist Irving Fisher told his audience that 'stock prices have reached what looks like a permanently high plateau'. But Fisher was wrong. Just over a week later, the market suffered its biggest-ever one-day sell-off: the first of a series of major losses that would become the Great Depression. By 1932, the US stock market was 89 per cent down from its 1929 peak.

Speculation was partly to blame for the crash. As share prices had risen, more people had piled into the market, hoping to get rich quickly. Businessman Joseph Kennedy, father of the future US president John F. Kennedy, apparently told friends that he knew something was amiss when talk of shares spread outside his usual circles: 'If the shoe-shine boys are giving stock tips, then it's time to get out of the market.' But few saw the crash coming. Many had borrowed to invest, and the resulting price drop left them penniless. Across the world, financial markets followed the US share market downwards.

Although four-fifths of the population did not own shares (stock-owning shoeshine boys may not have been so common after all), the market crash swiftly had an impact on the rest of the economy. Businesses stopped investing. Frightened citizens stopped spending. In turn, less consumption meant less economic activity. Millions lost their jobs. In the United States, unemployment peaked at 25 per cent, meaning that one in four workers who wanted a job were unable to find one. Tent cities sprang up in London's Hyde Park, New York's

Central Park and the Sydney Domain. Latin America was especially hard hit by the Depression, which contributed to the rise of authoritarian nationalism. In 1930, miliary juntas seized power in Argentina and Brazil.

The Great Depression was felt around the world.

Studying the problem of the Great Depression, British economist John Maynard Keynes argued that the problem occurred because people's actions affected one another in unexpected ways. Keynes likened the problem to a situation in which members of a bee colony decide that they will live thrifty lives. Thrift might seem virtuous, but because one bee's consumption is another's production, the colony collapses and all the bees in their hollow tree are left miserable. Keynes argued that the solution was for the government to spend money – ideally on public works projects – to restart the economy.

This was not a universal view among economists. Perhaps the most articulate exponent of the alternative perspective was Austrian economist Friedrich von Hayek. Hayek saw economic downturns as a necessary evil. He believed that government policies in the pre-crisis period made interest rates too low, which led firms to borrow unwisely. When the crisis came, it was those imprudent firms that collapsed. A recession was less like an avoidable illness and more like the inevitable hangover that follows a drinking binge.[4]

It isn't hard to see the moral messages behind these two analyses. To Hayek, recessions represented a clean-out of bad investments. Keynes saw recessions as painful and unnecessary. Hayek believed that government intervention would only make things worse. Keynes thought that government had a valuable role in smoothing the economic cycle. Hayek feared that democratic governments could erode liberty and believed that transitional dictatorships were sometimes necessary.

The differences between these two economists extended to their personal lives. Hayek was the more austere figure, raised by emotionally distant parents at a time when Austria was losing on the battlefield and suffering economically. He was cold and reserved; one biography reckons he had only three close male friends in his life.[5]

In contrast, Keynes was brimming with self-belief. He had learnt economics in his spare time, and when he underperformed in an exam he cheerfully opined, 'I evidently knew more about economics than my examiners.'[6] Keynes was a collector of Picassos, Renoirs and Matisses, and an investor who was a multimillionaire by today's standards. He kept diaries of his sexual exploits (with men and women), recording sixty-five encounters in 1909, twenty-six in 1910, thirty-nine in 1911 and so on.[7] Indeed, his broad tastes may have contributed to Keynes's open-mindedness and liberal world view. Keynes had a knack for friendship and both he and his wife, Lydia, were members of the Bloomsbury Group, a clique of English writers and painters. Another member of that group, writer Virginia Woolf, described Keynes as 'a gorged seal' with a 'double chin, ledge of red lip' and 'little eyes'. He was cosmopolitan, optimistic and confident, qualities that helped make him the most influential economist of the early twentieth century.

The Keynes–Hayek difference was summed up in a mock rap battle penned by video producer John Papola and economist Russ Roberts. The chorus goes:

> *We've been going back and forth for a century*
> *[Keynes] I want to steer markets,*
> *[Hayek] I want them set free*
> *There's a boom-and-bust cycle and good reason*
> *to fear it*
> *[Hayek] Blame low interest rates.*
> *[Keynes] No . . . it's the animal spirits*

Keynesians thought recessions were like natural disasters: a shock that could hit any of us. Modern policymakers are largely Keynesian (although we differ in how big the government response to shocks should be). One critic of Hayek argued that his approach to recessions was 'as unsuitable as denying blankets and stimulants to a drunk who has fallen into an icy pond, on the grounds that his original problem was overheating'.[8] Hayek's influence on mainstream economics today is not through his views on managing the business cycle, but from his writings on 'the invisible hand' of the market, which note how spontaneous order can emerge from a free market in which individuals are pursuing their own self-interest.

The 1930s Depression is referred to as the 'Great' Depression partly because it lasted so long. Rather than listen to Keynes, some nations pursued austerity – cutting government budgets in the face of the downturn. According to one study, unemployment in 1939 – a decade after the stock market crash – was above 10 per cent in Belgium, Canada, Denmark, the Netherlands, Norway and the United Kingdom.[9] For many households, incomes after inflation were lower in 1939 than they had been a decade earlier.

One of the factors that prolonged the Great Depression was a retreat from openness. In 1930, US Republicans Reed Smoot and Willis Hawley co-sponsored legislation to increase tariffs on over 20,000 agricultural and industrial imports. Demonstrating their profession's commitment to free trade, 1,028 economists wrote an open letter urging President Herbert Hoover to veto the *Smoot-Hawley Tariff Act*. Demonstrating the tendency of politicians to ignore economists on trade matters, the president signed it into law.

The increase in tariffs hurt United States firms by raising the prices of many of their inputs. Hundreds of car parts were targeted, which harmed the automotive industry. The tariff on wool rags was more than doubled, damaging textile manufacturers who used wool rags to make cheap clothing.[10] Other countries responded with fresh tariffs of their own.[11] French increases in car tariffs virtually closed its market to mid-priced US vehicles. Spain raised tariffs on many products exported by the US, including sewing machines, razor blades and tyres. Canada raised tariffs and imposed 'anti-dumping' duties.

Immigration restrictions tightened in the years following the end of World War I.[12] Canada banned migration from some of the countries it had fought against. The US Congress passed immigration restrictions that effectively banned all migrants from Asia and reduced national quotas from other countries. Policies were tightened further still in the 1930s. Australia imposed an immigration fee equivalent to one-quarter of the average annual Australian wage. Thailand introduced a literacy test and expensive residence permits. New Zealand closed its Department of Immigration. Migration from Europe was lower in the 1930s than it had been in the mid-1800s.

The Depression also led to a significant slowdown in international capital flows. In prior decades, investment flowed from high-income to low-income countries, chasing higher returns, and often following migrant flows. Both the supply of foreign investment and the demand for overseas investment dropped. From Vietnam to Brazil, a wave of foreign investment in the first three decades of the century began to peter out in the 1930s.[13]

Yet the Depression also helped create the political conditions for progressive reform. One of its key architects was workers' rights advocate Frances Perkins. Early in her career, Perkins witnessed the Triangle Shirtwaist Factory fire in New York City, in which 146 workers – most of them young migrant women – were killed by a fire in a city building where the exits had been locked to prevent workers taking unauthorised breaks. The experience caused Perkins to take a job working for the City of New York, where she championed safer workplaces and a cap on the maximum number of hours that women and children could work.

In 1933, newly elected president Franklin D. Roosevelt appointed Frances Perkins as the US Secretary of Labor, making her the first woman to hold a cabinet post. Perkins helped design the *United States Social Security Act*, a key part of Roosevelt's New Deal. Enacted in 1935, social security provided direct payments to the elderly, and over the coming decades dramatically reduced aged poverty. Although it was funded by payroll taxes, social security allowed people to get back more than they contributed. Its first monthly beneficiary, Vermont schoolteacher Ida Fuller, began receiving benefits in 1940, when she retired after having paid US$25 in social security taxes. Fuller lived to age 100, collecting a total of US$22,889. Accounting for inflation, her benefits were over 200 times what she had paid in taxes.

President Roosevelt signs the *Social Security Act* in 1935, with Frances Perkins in attendance.

The 1930s also saw considerable progress in the way that economists thought about market failure. No one was more crucial to that work than Joan Robinson. Robinson grew up in a family that valued unorthodox thinking and nonconformity, and joined the faculty of Cambridge University in 1931. While Keynes dominated macroeconomics at the time, Robinson's focus was on microeconomics, and testing some of Alfred Marshall's analysis.

In 1933, Robinson published *The Economics of Imperfect Competition*, which flipped economic thinking about the way markets typically operate. Marshall's models had tended to assume an economy in which markets were composed of many buyers and many sellers. That might be a fine depiction of a few sectors, such as the stock market. But what about the British East India Company? Robinson's work presented vigorous competition not as the normal state of affairs but as a special case. Where others imagined a dynamic marketplace with lots of traders, Robinson's analysis recognised that monopolies and oligopolies were common.

Robinson also introduced the concept of monopsony: the situation in which a seller has pricing power over its suppliers. In a one-company town, the employer has monopsony power over workers, allowing it to pay them less than their true value. If a supermarket chain controls most of the grocery sector, it can exert monopsony power over farmers, paying them less than they would receive in a competitive market.

Robinson's relentless curiosity meant that she was constantly questioning ideas – including her own. Thirty-six years after *The Economics of Imperfect Competition* came out, she wrote a harsh eight-page critique of her own book, then made it the preface to the second edition. Yet despite her significant intellectual contributions, Robinson was not made a full professor until 1965. Perhaps not coincidentally, that was the year her husband retired from Cambridge. In 1975, there were such strong rumours that she would win the Nobel Prize that *Businessweek* published a long profile of her work ahead of the announcement. But the prize went elsewhere.

We take it for granted today that economists can calculate economic output, but modern national accounts did not emerge until the 1920s and 1930s. The goal was to obtain an accurate series over time of production and expenditure, which would make it possible to determine changes in the total income of a nation. In the United Kingdom, Arthur Bowley and Josiah Stamp attempted a comprehensive analysis of a single year. A.E. Feavearyear followed up with a study examining how the British national income was spent – looking separately at everything from rabbits to religious donations. Another statistical pioneer was Colin Clark, who had a successful career at Cambridge University and an unsuccessful tilt at politics (he stood for the British Labour Party on three occasions), before moving to Australia, publishing pathbreaking estimates of national income. In the United States, Simon Kuznets and the National Bureau of Economic Research (founded in 1920) played a leading role in systematising the collection of national statistics on prices, earnings, savings and profits. For academics, the collection of data facilitated research. For policymakers, measuring economic output facilitated timely interventions to avoid recession.

The way that official statistics are handled by autocracies is a reminder that we should not take the role of statisticians for granted. In 1937, Joseph Stalin announced that the Soviet Union would conduct a census – the first for more than a decade. Stalin had been boasting that under his policies the population was growing rapidly – adding more people each year than the entire population of Finland. It was a lie. His policies had caused famine and mass emigration, and the census results showed a population that was at least 10 million people smaller than Stalin had claimed. The 1937 census also showed that most of the population were religious, a result at odds with the anti-religious views of the leadership. Stalin ordered that the results not be published. The chief of the census bureau, Olimpiy Kvitkin, was executed.

SADIE ALEXANDER

The first African American woman to receive a doctorate in economics was Sadie Alexander, whose parents had both been enslaved. Alexander's dissertation, written at the University of Pennsylvania, focused on Black families that had migrated north to Philadelphia. Through interviews with one hundred families, she analysed living standards and spending patterns. Though many lived in overcrowded homes, Alexander found, two-thirds got by without any outside assistance – particularly if they bought goods in bulk and managed to avoid paying higher prices because they were Black.

Graduating in 1921, Alexander was unable to find a job in economics befitting her ability. She returned to Penn to study law, then joined her husband's firm – working together on civil rights lawsuits to desegregate Philadelphia's cinemas and hotels. But her public speeches are rich in economic insights.[14] In one, she noted how policies to help poor whites inadvertently harmed African Americans. When President Franklin D. Roosevelt's 1933 *National Industrial Recovery Act* boosted wages in certain sectors, employers in those industries fired Black workers and hired whites in their place. Alexander dubbed the law 'the Negro Reduction Act'.

To achieve racial equality, Alexander argued, full employment was essential. Because Black workers were 'the last to be hired and the first to be fired', they suffered most in an economic slump. Full employment also improved racial attitudes. Alexander argued that full employment strengthened democracy by ameliorating white workers' 'fears of economic rivalry'. In a strong labour market, Alexander contended, political demagogues were less likely to find a foothold. She was ahead of her time: recent research shows that economic crises raise the odds that right-wing populists win office.[15]

8

WORLD WAR II AND BRETTON WOODS

AS FASCISM ROSE, THE ALLIES mistakenly attempted to appease Hitler. The 1938 Munich Agreement allowed Germany to annexe the Sudetenland. The 1939 Nazi–Soviet Pact facilitated Germany's invasion of Eastern Europe. Economic factors mattered too. Japan's imperial ambitions were partly a product of its lack of domestic energy reserves. Hyperinflation and the burden of World War I reparations caused resentment among many Germans. Germany's invasion of Russia represented an attempt to gain control of additional oil reserves in the region between the Black Sea and the Caspian Sea.[1]

Economics also suggests that the outcome of World War II could have been predicted from the fundamentals. Just as with the US Civil War and World War I, the balance of resources at the outset strongly favoured the eventual winner. Compared with the Axis powers (Germany, Italy, Japan and their allies), the Allied powers (the United Kingdom, France and their allies) had more than twice as many people, more than seven times as much territory, and a combined income that was 40 per cent higher.[2]

Germany's early victories owed much to the skill of generals such as Erwin Rommel, and tactics such as *blitzkrieg* (lightning war) and *bewegungskrieg* (manoeuvre warfare). As one economic historian puts it, 'Everybody – the Poles, the Dutch, the Belgians, the French, the Yugoslavs, the Greeks, the British, the Americans, and the Russians – who faced the Nazis failed more or less equally, both tactically and operationally, at least in their initial encounters, and in no small number of subsequent encounters.'[3]

Yet there were no decisive battles in World War II.[4] Not Pearl Harbor. Not Midway. Not Stalingrad. Not Kursk. The war was primarily a contest of industrial production, and the Allied powers had more resources at their disposal. This was true even midway through the war, because while Hitler's Germany had annexed much of Europe, the United States and the Soviet Union had joined the conflict on the side of the Allies. In 1942, the Allied powers still retained a decisive advantage in people, territory and income. Aircraft carriers illustrate the differential: although Japan grasped their strategic value early, the Allied powers built nine-tenths of the carriers produced during the war.

The combatant nations differed in how much of their economy they devoted to the war effort.[5] Italy never devoted more than one-quarter of its economy to World War II, while at its peak Japan was devoting more than three-quarters of its economy to the military. The United Kingdom and Russia also managed to deliver more than half of their output to the war, while the United States devoted two-fifths of its economy to the war. Put together, this gave a substantial advantage to the Allied powers. When it came to the production of munitions, the Allied powers produced at least twice as many rifles, tanks, aircraft, mortars and warships. The Axis powers were literally outgunned.

Over the course of the war, the economic damage of World War II was more devastating than that of World War I, largely because the technology of killing had advanced so much in the intervening years. In the air, World War I's biplanes and zeppelins played a relatively minor role, while World War II saw squadrons of bombers devastate cities with incendiary – and, ultimately, atomic – bombs. On the oceans, World War II featured aircraft carriers, enabling naval battles in which the opposing ships never saw one another. Long-range bombers, jet fighters, self-guiding torpedoes and cruise missiles all emerged from World War II. All up, World War II claimed three times as many lives as World War I had done.

As well as new inventions, World War II brought advances in econometrics – the application of statistical techniques to economic questions. One practical concern was how best to reinforce bombers to increase their chances of surviving enemy fire. Naive colleagues had looked at the underside of returning aircraft and, seeing disproportionate damage to places like the tail, had suggested reinforcing those spots. But mathematician Abraham Wald, a Jewish refugee from Hungary, recognised that they were only seeing part of the picture.

What they saw was the damage that a bomber could sustain and still return home. The absence of returning bombers with nose damage suggested that it was precisely spots like this that required additional reinforcement. Wald's techniques continue to be used by econometricians today.

What was missing from the data? Every plane that had been shot down.

The peace that followed World War II was more enduring partly because countries learnt the lessons of the previous conflict. Through the Marshall Plan, the United States provided US$13 billion to Western Europe, equating to around 3 per cent of the region's annual economic output.[6] In Germany and Japan, the occupying powers placed considerable emphasis on restoration, with the result that both became major industrial powers within a generation.

Economists played a central role in building an international economic architecture that would sustain peace. In 1944, a conference in Bretton Woods, New Hampshire, brought together representatives from all forty-four Allied nations. It was a curious gathering. Keynes represented the

United Kingdom, hoping to avoid the economic mistakes that had been made after World War I. The United States was represented by Harry Dexter White, who is rumoured to have been a Russian spy. France was represented by Pierre Mendès France, which must have made things easy for those writing out the name cards.

Out of this unlikely gathering came an agreement to end economic isolationism, and an acceptance that trade and capital flows would make for a richer and more stable world. Bretton Woods led to the creation of the World Bank, which sought to raise living standards in the poorest nations, and the International Monetary Fund, which aimed to help countries avoid financial crises. The Bretton Woods Agreement partially restored the gold standard, with one US dollar fixed to 1/35th of an ounce of gold, and other countries' currencies pegged to the US dollar. However, the ability to convert banknotes into gold was restricted to official international transactions, and rarely occurred in practice.

Macroeconomists in the post-war years continued to build on the work of Keynes. One larger-than-life figure was Bill Phillips. Born on a New Zealand dairy farm, Phillips worked as a cinema manager, gold miner and crocodile hunter before training as an engineer and enlisting in World War II, where he spent three years in a Japanese concentration camp. While incarcerated, Phillips learnt Chinese from other prisoners, and helped build a secret radio. After the war, he enrolled to study sociology at the London School of Economics, but soon switched to economics. In 1949, working in his landlady's garage, Phillips used water pumps to build a hydraulic model of the economy.[7] Designed initially as a teaching aid, the machine turned out to be good at simulating the effect of potential policy changes – showing how changing government spending and taxation affects the 'circular flow' of income. Around a dozen were built, including one at the University of Cambridge that remains operational to this day.

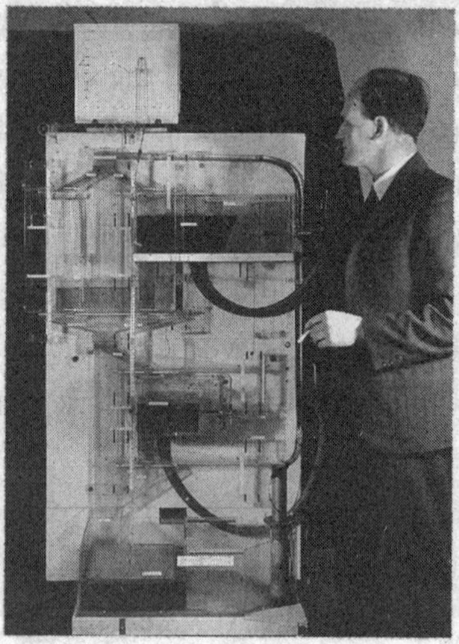

Bill Phillips with his Monetary National Income Analogue Computer (MONIAC).

Advances on Keynes's models were developed by the Massachusetts Institute of Technology's Paul Samuelson. Samuelson's 'pragmatic Keynesianism' argued that sticky prices and wages prevented full employment from being achieved purely through the market, providing an economic justification for government intervention in times of crisis. While economists tend to communicate mostly through articles rather than books, textbooks are important, and Samuelson's 1948 textbook is one of the most important of them all. Samuelson thought that Keynes's book *The General Theory of Employment, Interest, and Money* was 'a work of genius', yet riddled with contradictions and poorly written. Samuelson believed that mathematics was the natural language of economics and set about formalising Keynes's ideas mathematically – in the process helping to move economics away from storytelling and towards equations. As Samuelson contentedly noted, 'I do not care who writes the nation's laws, so long as I can write its textbooks.'

One of the ideas emphasised in Samuelson's textbook was comparative advantage, a principle articulated by David Ricardo more than a century earlier. Comparative advantage shows that when two countries trade with one another, both stand to benefit. Difference is what makes trade work. Countries trade because certain crops grow better in different parts of the world, because some nations have developed a knack of producing particular products, or because lower wage levels make labour-intensive goods cheaper to manufacture. Brazilian coffee, Swiss clocks and Bangladeshi textiles each represent a difference embodied in an export. Later in his career, Samuelson described comparative advantage as the best example in the social sciences of a proposition that is both true and not obvious.

Many policymakers had forgotten this insight in the 1930s, as the *Smoot-Hawley Tariff Act* sparked a rise in protectionism and a fall in trade volumes. But after World War II, trade began to grow again. In 1947, countries representing more than four-fifths of global trade signed up to the General Agreement on Tariffs and Trade. Between them, they agreed to reduce 45,000 tariffs, affecting US$10 billion of world trade.

World War II was a powerful spur in the expansion of the welfare state. Governments raised taxes, introduced rationing of food and clothing and provided family payments. The memory of the Depression and the suffering on the battlefield led many to believe that after the peace it was time to build a fairer society. In the United Kingdom, economists Janet and William Beveridge produced a key report in 1942 that identified five evils – squalor, ignorance, want, idleness and disease – and proposed a national insurance scheme that would provide for those who were unemployed, sick or elderly. The philosophy underpinning the Beveridge Report differed from Bismarck's reforms: where Bismarck's was about individual contributions, the Beveridge approach entailed a universal government program. So powerful was the demand for this kind of social program that the British people threw the Churchill government out of office in 1945, electing a Labour government that promised a social safety net that would provide for its citizens 'from the cradle to the grave'.

This expansion of the welfare state paralleled an increase in the role of government in the economy. Across advanced nations, the government's share of the economy grew from an average of 24 per cent in 1937 to 28 per cent in 1960.[8] After the end of World War II, the United Kingdom nationalised its railways, coal mines, electricity supply industry, much of the iron and steel sector and the Bank of England. France nationalised the car company Renault, which had collaborated with Nazi occupiers, as well as the gas and electricity industry and most of the banking and insurance sectors. New Zealand nationalised the Bank of New Zealand. Sweden concluded the process of nationalising its railways.

Across the advanced world, the increasing role of government was reflected in a higher tax take. Prior to World War II, the average worker in many countries did not pay income tax. World War II saw income taxes expanded to cover most workers. This was facilitated by the introduction of pay-as-you-go taxation, which required employers to deduct income taxes and remit them to the government. Workers could always find out how much tax they had paid, but were less likely to resent losing the money if they never saw it in the first place.

9

THE GLORIOUS THIRTY?

ONE OF THE STRIKING THINGS about life is how much of it is determined by luck. At the moment your parents got together, the odds that the particular sperm and ovum that created you would join up was less than one in a million. Worldwide, most of the differences in income are determined by a person's country of birth and the social position of their parents.[1] Unless you think you got to pick your parents, that's luck too.

In the job market, luck is all around us. A young person who finishes high school during a recession will find it harder to get a job – a 'scarring' effect that can persist for a decade or more. Some workers pick promising careers, only to find that technology has made them jobless. When a large firm in a small town goes bust, it can be near-impossible for everyone to find work in the same area. There's the misfortune of disability – from congenital anomalies to workplace injuries – that can make it difficult for a person to earn enough to support themselves. And there's the possibility that a person lives longer than their savings will last – a lucky outcome in terms of enjoying more years, but an unlucky one in a society that doesn't provide for its elderly.

In the post-war era, redistribution from the lucky to the unlucky occurred through both the welfare system and the tax system. Income taxes were highly progressive – meaning that top earners paid a higher percentage of their income. The Beatles song 'Taxman' had the collector giving 'one for you' and keeping 'nineteen for me'. They weren't exaggerating. At that time, members of the band were in the top tax bracket, which made them subject to a 95 per cent supertax. Above that threshold, nineteen out of every twenty dollars the band made was paid in tax. Some years later, the Rolling Stones decamped from Britain to avoid tax, calling the resulting album *Exile on Main St*.

In the workforce, unions had become an increasingly powerful force, affecting virtually every aspect of working life. The way unions operated could be strikingly different. In Sweden, trade union federations negotiated national wage agreements with central employer bodies. In Australia, unions argued wage cases before industrial tribunals. In the United States, unions bargained directly with company management. In countries that were still ruled by colonial powers, unions were often at the vanguard of national independence movements and campaigns for greater local control. Across the world, sick leave, holiday leave, weekend pay loadings, safety standards, anti-discrimination laws, job security and pay itself have all been shaped by unions. Whether or not you are a union member, it is likely that your job would look quite different if unions had never existed.

Trade unions campaigned for higher wages, safer working conditions and anti-discrimination laws.

The post-war decades saw unions grow strongly in many advanced nations. By the 1970s, one in three employees in the OECD group of advanced nations were union members (today, the figure is less than one in six).[2] The strength of unions in the post-war era was partly a function of the structure of the economy. One way to think about unionisation is as a contest between employees to organise together across a workplace, and employers to establish new workplaces. This helps explain why unionisation rates tend to be higher in factories and the public sector than in start-up enterprises. In many nations, a strong manufacturing sector proved fertile ground for union organising, which in turn ensured good wages in these jobs.

During the 1950s and 1960s, manufacturing offered a pathway to the middle class for workers with little formal education.

Yet formal education was just what many workers were acquiring during this period, as school completion rates rose and tertiary education became increasingly common. This was a major factor in the reduction of inequality that occurred in many advanced nations during the post-war decades. One theory of inequality is that it depends on the relative growth in education and technology.[3] If education stagnates while technology advances, society tends to become more unequal. When the level of education grows faster than new technologies emerge, society becomes more equal. The best way of reducing inequality, according to this theory, is by ensuring that everyone gets a great education.

Another grand theory of inequality – not inconsistent with the idea of a race between education and technology – focuses on the difference between the rate of economic growth (g) and the rate of return on capital investment (r). Capital assets such as land and corporate equity tend to be skewed towards the most affluent (the top 10 per cent today own 76 per cent of global wealth), so a high return on capital disproportionately benefits the richest.[4] In his book *Capital in the Twenty-First Century*, French economist Thomas Piketty proposed that when $r > g$, inequality rises. This, he argued, is the normal state of human affairs.

In the post-war decades, by contrast, the rate of return on capital in many advanced countries was dramatically below its long-run average, while the rate of economic growth was significantly above its historic average. With r < g, inequality in many high-income countries fell. Across the advanced world, jobs were plentiful, wages rose faster than profits, and earnings rose faster on the factory floor than in the corner office.

The effect may have been widespread, but each nation took pride in its success. The French called the three post-war decades *les Trente Glorieuses*. The Italians referred to *il boom economico*. The Spanish dubbed it *el milagro económico español* (the Spanish economic miracle). Germans called it *das Wunder am Rhein* (the Miracle on the Rhine). My own research shows that voters were more likely to re-elect governments that had delivered high economic growth, but that voters were not very good at distinguishing between governments that were lucky enough to hold office when the world economy was strong and those that were skilful enough to outperform the global average.[5]

The glorious decades didn't just create lucky politicians. This was the era when many Europeans got cars for the first time and many Americans bought their first freezer. Televisions and record players proliferated. One of the chief drivers of wealth equalisation was the spread of home ownership. For example, when World War I came to an end, 23 per cent of the British housing stock was owner-occupied. By the late 1970s, the figure had risen to nearly 58 per cent.[6]

The post-war decades also saw the large-scale entry of women into the paid workforce. Non-economists often attribute this to evolving social norms. But economists point also to the role of technology and policy. Electric stoves, vacuum cleaners, running water, refrigerators and washing machines simplified household work, transforming many women's lives. The contraceptive pill allowed women greater control over when to have children. As economists such as Claudia Goldin have pointed out, this in turn created a stronger incentive for women to invest in education.

For entrepreneurs, franchising created a new hybrid – a cross between setting up an independent small business and buying shares in a large firm. In 1953, Richard and Maurice McDonald sold their first franchise in Phoenix, Arizona. The following year, hard-driving businessman Ray Kroc used the franchising model to eventually grow McDonald's into the largest restaurant chain in the world.

An early McDonald's restaurant from the 1950s.

Hotels, supermarkets and real estate agents are also significant users of franchising. The model allows outlets to benefit from national advertising campaigns and standardised production processes, but also loads much of the risk onto the small franchisee, who may be at a negotiating disadvantage when dealing with the large franchisor.

The uptake of new technologies created unexpected effects. In 1955, one in fifty US homes had an air conditioner. By 1980, a majority did. Air conditioning spread rapidly around the world (there are now more than two billion air conditioners globally). The technology enabled a mass migration towards the equator in many advanced countries. Americans moved to Florida. Australians moved to Queensland. Equatorial and desert cities such as Singapore, Dubai and Doha boomed. Air conditioning literally rearranged the world.[7]

The spread of economics into other disciplines can be traced to this era. One day, economist Gary Becker found himself running late for a meeting.[8] If he parked legally, he realised, he would be late. Only by illegally parking could he arrive at the meeting on time. Becker calculated the chance of getting caught, multiplied it by the fine, and decided that the expected cost was smaller than the expected benefit of getting to the meeting on time. The experience led him to produce a seminal article: 'Crime and punishment: An economic approach'.[9] Rather than assuming that criminals are stupid, Becker reasoned, why not think about how they would behave if they were trying to maximise their wellbeing like everyone else? One implication of this work is that deterrence depends on both the penalty and the odds of detection. If potential criminals place little value on the long term, then doubling police patrols might be a more cost-effective way to reduce street crime than doubling jail sentences.

Becker's work also brought the tools of economics to the study of discrimination.[10] Racist employers, he reasoned, will end up paying a bigger wage bill. By refusing to hire minority job applicants, racist employers are narrowing the pool of people they are willing to employ. So to get the same calibre of employees, they will end up paying more than a non-racist employer. In a competitive market, in which customers do not share the employer's prejudices, being a racist will lead to lower profits. Becker's work implies that greater competition will put the economic squeeze on racist employers – providing an economic incentive for them to choose the best candidate for the job. The same holds for other forms of discrimination, including against women, older workers, religious minorities, people with disabilities and LGBTIQA+ people. Competition alone will not eliminate discrimination, but it can play a positive role.

During this period, applied economics also continued to advance. One key area was in separating correlation from causation. People with big shoes tend to be taller, but wearing larger shoes won't make you grow. People who eat ice cream are more likely to get sunburnt, but passing up a cold treat on a hot day won't protect you from skin cancer. In the realm of economics, it is tricky to determine the impact of foreign aid on economic growth (since aid is often directed towards countries in distress), or to disentangle the impact of exporting on company performance (since better-managed firms often have a more global outlook).

THE SHIPPING CONTAINER

In the early 1950s, docks were covered with an assortment of cartons, drums and crates. Loading a ship might involve hauling coils of steel wire, loose pieces of timber, bales of cotton and barrels of olives. Cargo was routinely damaged. Workers were often injured or killed. Getting everything onto a ship could take days. The expense of loading and unloading ships sometimes accounted for half the total transport costs. For many goods, international trade was out of the question.

The largest ships can carry over 10,000 containers.

The inventor of the modern shipping container was US trucking entrepreneur Malcolm McLean. On 26 April 1956, McLean put fifty-eight containers aboard the SS *Ideal* X, and sailed them from New Jersey to Texas. His containers had a twistlock mechanism above each corner, allowing the containers to be easily moved using cranes. Over the coming decades, McLean and others in the transport industry debated the specifications, finally settling on a standard. Today, a majority of the world's shipping containers measure 12.2 metres long by 2.4 metres wide by 2.6 metres high. Each container can typically carry 30 tonnes. Modern container ships are hundreds of metres long and carry thousands of containers. Loading or unloading takes a few hours, managed by computer systems that ensure the ship remains stable throughout.

The standardised shipping container has reduced freight costs so much that they barely factor. A standardised steel box brought the world closer together.

In laboratory science, researchers have control over what is in each test tube, but things are messier when dealing with people in the real world. Yet medicine had begun to shift towards randomised trials. Shortly after the end of World War II, researchers tested tuberculosis treatments and the polio vaccine by comparing them against patients who had been randomly selected to receive a placebo. Social scientists saw how they could use similar techniques. In 1962, randomised policy trials took a significant step forward, with the commencement of two social experiments testing early childhood interventions. The Early Training Project in Tennessee and the Perry Preschool Project in Michigan evaluated whether high-quality early childhood programs could make a difference for extremely disadvantaged preschoolers.

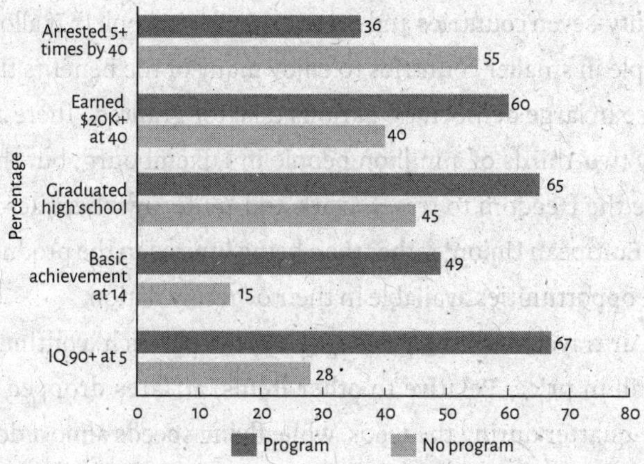

The Perry Preschool Project's randomised trial showed large differences between the 'program' group and the 'no program' control group.

By the time the participants reached adulthood, the differences were clear, with those who had received early intervention recording higher incomes and lower arrest rates than their counterparts in the control group. These programs not only reshaped economists' thinking about early childhood, but also contributed to the growing interest in randomisation as a tool to separate correlation from causation.

Economic integration continued to increase during the post-war decades. Following the creation of the General Agreement on Tariffs and Trade, countries signed significant tariff deals in 1949, 1951, 1956, 1962, 1967, 1979 and 1994. The European Economic Community was formed in 1957, removing all tariffs between its six founding members, and steadily attracting more members over the coming decades. Today, the European Union is the world's most significant trading bloc, comprising twenty-seven countries and over 400 million people.[11] It allows people in smaller countries to enjoy many of the benefits that those in large democratic nations take for granted. There are only two-thirds of a million people in Luxembourg, but they have the freedom to travel, work and trade anywhere across the European Union, rather than being limited to the products and opportunities available in their own tiny nation.

Air travel, once the privilege of the super-rich, continued to fall in price. Relative to other items, airfares dropped by one-quarter during the 1960s, while flying speeds almost doubled.[12] The year 1970 saw the introduction of the Boeing 747, the first wide-bodied aircraft, which could carry around 400 passengers. Growing demand for flights led to another problem:

passengers often paid for their tickets at the airport, and slow credit card processing caused some travellers to miss their planes. In 1970, American Airlines, IBM and American Express conducted the first trial of a magnetic stripe credit card at Chicago's O'Hare airport. The technology simplified air travel, and the retail experience more broadly. It also encouraged the growth of personal debt. Median credit card debts today exceed US$300 in India, US$1,500 in China and US$5,000 in the United States.[13] A plethora of studies have shown that when people pay with credit cards rather than cash, they are more prone to overspending – making decisions that they later regret.[14]

One reason we may regret a purchase is that many goods drop in value the moment we leave the store. In 1970, economist George Akerlof explained why.[15] Suppose sellers of used cars know whether they have a high-quality car (a 'peach'), or a low-quality car (a 'lemon'). Buyers do not know this information. This causes sellers of lemons to flood the market. Knowing they are likely to get a lemon, buyers are only willing to pay lemon prices. So peach owners don't sell, and the used-car market becomes 'a market for lemons'. The research, which would eventually earn Akerlof the Nobel Prize, was rejected by three journals before being published – a fact that continues to provide consolation to economists whose work is rejected (the rejection rate in the top five economics journals is now around 95 per cent).[16]

The prosperity of this period wasn't universal. After Mao Zedong's Chinese Communist Party took power in 1949, many business leaders were executed. Agriculture was collectivised, reducing the incentive for peasant farmers to work hard because any additional produce from their labours had to be shared across the entire community. In 1958, Mao launched the 'Great Leap Forward', a madcap plan in which farmers were encouraged to produce iron and steel in backyard furnaces. Millions of perfectly good pots and pans were melted into scrap iron.

In the same year, Mao demanded that people eliminate sparrows, on the basis that they ate grain. The campaign called on people to make so much noise that the sparrows died of exhaustion. Millions of sparrows died, which meant that they were not around to eat the locusts that devoured much of the following year's crop. Eventually, Mao imported 250,000 sparrows from the Soviet Union to restore the ecosystem. Crop losses contributed to a 40 per cent drop in rice and wheat output between 1957 and 1961, and a famine that killed tens of millions.[17]

More chaos was to come. Starting in 1966, the Cultural Revolution empowered Mao's Red Guards, who attacked scientists, scholars and intellectuals. Universities and schools were closed, and millions of urban youths (including future president Xi Jinping) were sent to live in the countryside – often missing out on any formal education. Ongoing political struggles left many parts of the government in disarray, contributing to tragedies such as the 1975 Banqiao Dam failure, which inundated at least five million homes, and killed tens of thousands of people. The result of Mao's policies can be seen by comparing the Chinese economy with its neighbours'. During Mao's time in office, real per capita incomes in Hong Kong grew twice as fast as in mainland China. South Korea grew four times faster than China. Japan grew five times faster.[18]

In Cuba, Fidel Castro led a revolution in 1959 that overthrew the government and established a communist dictatorship. The government took over significant sectors of the economy, broke up large landholdings, and redistributed agricultural land to peasants. Over the decade after the Cuban revolution, living standards flatlined. Castro and his fellow revolutionaries knew little about economics. According to one (possibly apocryphal) story, at a late-night meeting of the leadership, Castro looked around the room and asked for 'a good economist' to become president of the National Bank of Cuba. A sleepy Che Guevara raised his hand. Surprised, Castro said, 'Che, I didn't know you were a good economist.' Guevera immediately apologised: 'Oh, I thought you asked for a good communist!'[19]

Elsewhere in Latin America, some countries began to shift away from global engagement. In Argentina, economist Raúl Prebisch advocated import substitution industrialisation, in which low-income countries sought to build up a manufacturing sector based around products for which there was substantial domestic demand. While comparative advantage trade theory implies that countries should specialise, import substitution suggests that countries could benefit from creating a diverse manufacturing base. Many advocates of import substitution also supported raising tariffs to discourage imports. This proved to be especially damaging when tariffs were imposed on goods that were themselves used for production, such as arc welders, tractors or office equipment. Import substitution industrialisation did not produce the hoped-for economic gains and would be largely abandoned by the final decades of the twentieth century.

In the decade after World War II, a wave of nations declared independence, including the Philippines, Jordan, Syria, Libya, Cambodia, Laos and Vietnam. The largest was India, which turned decisively away from capitalism. A clunky centralised planning system, rampant corruption and a lack of trade with the world contributed to what was dubbed 'the Hindu rate of growth'. Jawaharlal Nehru, India's prime minister from 1947 to 1964, had been influenced by what he saw when he visited the Soviet Union and was determined that the government should heavily regulate the economy. Nehru initiated a series of 'Five Year Plans', modelled on the Soviet system. India's 'licence raj' meant that up to eighty agencies had to be satisfied before a firm could commence operations.[20] The Indian government would often then decide what was produced, and at what price it would be sold. This approach constrained innovation and reduced productivity growth.

Yet unlike China, India experienced no famines in the period after independence in 1947. One theory for this was developed by Indian economist Amartya Sen, who witnessed the 1943 Bengal Famine as a nine-year-old child – helping to hand out rice to victims of a disaster that ultimately killed

Hungry citizens waiting in line at a soup kitchen during the 1943 Bengal Famine.

around three million people while the country was under British rule. Sen argued that famines are not simply about food production; they can also be caused when governments divert food away from where it is needed. Democracies with a free press, Sen concluded, are extremely unlikely to suffer a famine. Sen's approach emphasises human capabilities – the ability to act in one's own interest. Human flourishing, he argues, is not merely about 'freedom from' (the freedom from interference by others) but also about the 'freedom to' (such as the freedom to get an education or actively participate in the democracy).

Sen has significantly influenced the United Nations' *Human Development Report*, which ranks countries on a broader set of indicators than economic output. In many cases, these metrics go together. Countries that are more democratic tend to enjoy more rapid rates of economic growth.[21] Nations with more rights for LGBTIQA+ people have higher incomes and higher rates of wellbeing.[22] Countries that encourage women to participate fully in society generally have higher living standards.[23]

The potential of markets to boost prosperity, and the importance of capabilities to human flourishing, can be seen in the trajectories of East and West Germany, and North and South Korea. After four decades of communist rule, living standards in East Germany were one-third of West German levels.[24] After almost eight decades of communism, living standards in North Korea are 1/23rd of the level in capitalist South Korea.[25] Both experiments also show that communism fails to encourage what Amartya Sen calls human capabilities. Along their shared border, it was the communist nation – not its capitalist counterpart – that built a wall and threatened to shoot its citizens if they tried to leave.

The late 1970s marked a turning point, in which many nations turned towards markets. For some, it led to the question of whether capitalism had gone too far. For others, the introduction of markets proved to be the difference between having enough to eat and going to bed hungry every night.

HUNGRY FOR CHANGE

History's worst famines include France in 1693–94, Ireland in 1740–41 and 1846–52, Finland in 1868, the Soviet Union in 1921–22 and Cambodia in 1975–79.[26] In each of these incidents, more than 5 per cent of the population died. Poor countries are most vulnerable to famines, as they have fewer resources to draw upon in hard times. Famines have often been precipitated by back-to-back harvest shortfalls, typically caused by extreme weather events. But they can be exacerbated by governmental failure. Totalitarian governments are more prone to making policy mistakes, concealing the true extent of the disaster, and refusing outside assistance.

Bridget O'Donnell and two of her children, who suffered during the 1846–52 Irish Potato Famine, which killed 12 per cent of the population.

When famine strikes, people are more likely to die from disease than actual starvation. The people most likely to die are the poorest, young children and the elderly. Women are less likely than men to die in famines, most likely due to the physiological fact that women's bodies have a higher fat-to-muscle ratio than men's.

Over time, the proportional death toll of famines has fallen. Even so, in the twentieth century, famines killed more people than the two world wars combined. Today, drastic crop failure need not lead to famine. The Food and Agriculture Organization and the World Food Programme, two United Nations bodies created to prevent famines, are generally able to provide food relief if they are allowed into a country. The danger of famine now comes from political risk more than agricultural risk. With good governance, the world can make famine history.

10

MARKETS, MARKETS EVERYWHERE

IN 1978, IN THE TINY Chinese village of Xiaogang, eighteen villagers met to sign a secret contract that could have cost them their lives. Like other parts of China, Xiaogang had suffered terribly during the Great Leap Forward. Out of a population of 120 people, more than half had died during the years from 1958 to 1960.[1] In the 1970s, people were still desperately hungry. They knew that agricultural output could be higher – but they also knew that the incentives of the collectivist system worked against it.

At that time, everything was owned by the collective. Yen Jingchang, one of those who signed the contract, summed it up by saying, 'Work hard, don't work hard – everyone gets the same. So people don't want to work.'[2] The contract, signed in a house with a mud floor and straw roof, went directly against the dictates of the communist authorities. It stated that each family would have its own plot of land and be allowed to keep part of the output. The agreement was so dangerous that the villagers also agreed to provide for each other's children if one was jailed or executed. The document, signed under an oil lamp, was hidden inside a piece of bamboo in the roof of one of the villagers, Yen Hongchang.

Yet it wasn't the document that gave them away, it was the fact that the output from private plots was so much higher. Previously, farmers had only started work on the collective farms at the sound of a whistle. Now, some began tending their private farms before sunrise. At the end of the year, Xiaogang's harvest was bigger than the previous five years combined. Local officials angrily interrogated Yen Hongchang. But he was lucky. China's new president, Deng Xiaoping, liked their ideas and encouraged other villagers to try similar experiments. Within a few years, Xiaogang's secret had become China's road out of poverty.

In the shift away from collectivisation, practice often outpaced laws. For example, it was not until 1988 that China legalised private businesses employing more than seven people.[3] Yet the transformation was rapid and its implications far-reaching. In the decade following the 1978 reforms, around 10 million Chinese – a number equivalent to the modern-day population of Sweden – were brought out of poverty every year.[4]

The changes were also a reminder of the economic tenet that societal changes tend to be driven more by technology and policy than social norms. Nowhere is the impact of policy clearer than with communist societies. Just as the Russian Revolution ushered in a collapse in living standards, the 1978 changes made the difference for millions of people between going hungry and having enough to eat. Since that year, economic growth in China has averaged over 9 per cent annually. Trade has been a critical component of this growth, allowing Chinese manufacturers to sell to a global market.

At the same time that China was increasing the role of the market, the United Kingdom and the United States were moving in a similar direction. The election of Margaret Thatcher in 1979 and Ronald Reagan in 1980 led to much less government intervention in the economy. In the United Kingdom, Thatcher privatised most of the utilities that had been in public hands. Public housing tenants were given the right to buy their properties – in the case of long-term tenants, at half the market value. More than one million public housing units were privatised. Home ownership initially rose, and then fell as many of the new owners onsold their homes to professional landlords.

In the United States, Reagan's eight years in office saw the top individual tax rate reduced from 70 per cent to 28 per cent. In the face of a strike by air traffic controllers, Reagan fired more than 10,000 workers, and hired non-union replacements. Business leaders followed his example. In the next few years, striking copper miners, meat packers, bus drivers and paper workers found themselves out of a job.[5] The power of unions began to wane. Reagan also reduced government regulation, easing price controls on cable television, ocean shipping, natural gas and interstate trucking services.[6]

An economist who advised both Thatcher and Reagan was the University of Chicago's Milton Friedman. Articulate and energetic, Milton Friedman and his wife Rose Friedman wrote popular books with titles such as *Capitalism and Freedom* and *Free to Choose*, created a ten-part television documentary on economics and penned regular newspaper articles. As a libertarian, Friedman believed in the primacy of freedom, which led him to oppose military conscription, support drug legalisation and advocate smaller government. Friedman criticised the claim that government payments could help economies avoid recession. Instead, he proposed a permanent income hypothesis, under which households anticipate that current government spending will need to be paid for by future tax increases. To spend is to tax, argued Friedman.

The permanent income hypothesis is elegant, but it does a poor job of describing how people actually behave. Either because people aren't perfectly rational or because they believe that government stimulus will grow the tax base, government spending can boost total economic activity. In practice, households do not cut back their spending in anticipation of future tax bills. Regardless of their political stripes, governments don't respond to recessions by sternly waggling their finger at the immorality of people who overextended their finances. Instead, they take the Keynesian approach of providing timely, targeted and temporary fiscal stimulus. As former central banker Mark Carney has noted, 'Just as there are no atheists in foxholes, there are no libertarians in financial crises.'[7]

Friedman was not the only influential 'Chicago School' economist in the 1980s. In competition policy, Robert Bork and Richard Posner argued for a more relaxed approach to corporate mergers, known as the consumer welfare standard.

Big could be beautiful, they claimed, pointing to instances in which larger firms produced their products more efficiently. During the 1980s, this strand of thought became increasingly dominant in the United States and around the world. What mattered, according to the Chicago School, was not whether a merger or a pricing policy harmed competitors but whether it could be shown to damage consumers. Under Reagan, competition laws were curtailed, and banks were given freedom to invest in a broader range of assets.

During the 1980s, many other advanced nations sought to downsize the public sector, cutting corporate tax rates and individual tax rates. A wave of privatisations swept the world, with governments in Europe, Asia and Latin America selling off state-owned enterprises such as telephone carriers, ports, toll roads, electricity producers and railways.[8] At the time, many economists believed that these enterprises would operate more efficiently under private ownership, where they would be subject to the rigours of the market and might face competitive pressure.

In practice, privatisation now appears to have been overhyped. In many cases, the assets that were privatised were natural monopolies, whose dominant position made them impervious to threat from competitors. Anyone who wants to compete against a privatised railway monopoly may have to invest millions of dollars in new tracks and trains – something likely to deter most new entrants. Selling a monopoly railway might bolster the government's coffers, but if it pushes up the price of train tickets over coming decades, it's a crummy deal.

In business school, budding CEOs learn about Michael Porter's 'five forces' that determine whether a firm can enjoy unusually high profits.[9] Industries get a big thumbs up from managers and investors when there is no competition, when potential entrants face barriers, when suppliers have little bargaining power, when customers have few alternatives, and when there is no threat of substitute products.

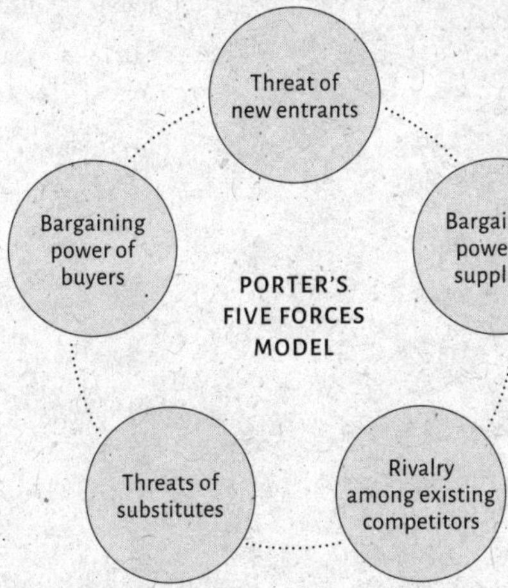

But while the five forces are good for profits, they're bad for consumers. Competition policy typically runs in precisely the opposite direction – towards boosting competition, encouraging new entrants and ensuring that monopolists do not abuse their power in their dealings with suppliers and customers. Short-sighted privatisations – as in the railway example above – often yielded a high initial sale price, but effectively levied a long-term tax on consumers, who ended up paying more to the privatised utility. Economists today tend to be more sceptical of privatisations that could lock in a monopoly provider.

BEAUTY PAYS

'Personal beauty', said Aristotle, 'is a greater recommendation than any letter of reference.' The economics of beauty studies the relationship between attractiveness and income. This is possible because while beauty is in the eye of the beholder, people behold it similarly. It turns out that if you ask multiple raters to assess a subject's attractiveness, they come up with comparable answers.

Crunching data from several surveys that include assessments of attractiveness and measures of earnings, economist Dan Hamermesh estimates that the best-looking workers make about 10 per cent more than the worst-lookers.[10] In advanced nations, this can add up to hundreds of thousands of dollars over a career. In general, the relationship between attractiveness and wages is stronger for men than for women. The beauty effect persists in occupations with little customer interaction, suggesting that employer discrimination against less attractive people may be at play. The phenomenon has been dubbed 'lookism', but few jurisdictions outlaw discrimination against people based on their physical appearance.

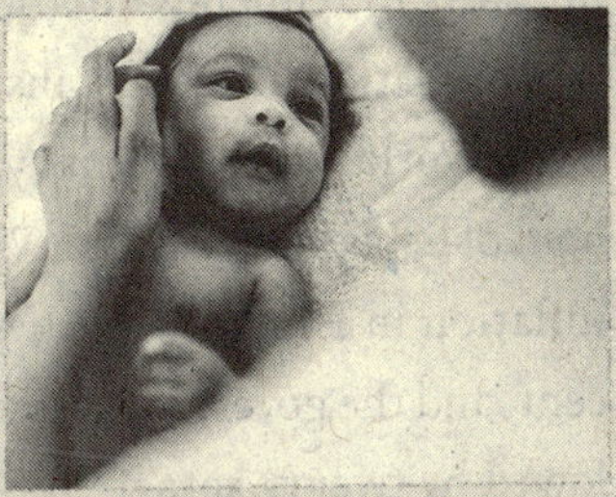

Babies stare longer at beautiful faces.

Beautiful people also benefit in other ways. Attractive people are also more likely to secure loans. Attractive political candidates are more likely to be elected. Attractive criminal defendants are more likely to be acquitted. Attractive students receive higher grades for their class presentations. Attractive professors – even economics professors – receive higher teaching evaluations. Even babies will gaze longer at attractive faces.

But don't fret if you're not gorgeous. Those who aren't conventionally comely should remember the theory of comparative advantage, and focus on their other strengths, such as brains, brawn and personality.

11

INFLATION TARGETING AND INEQUALITY

DURING THE 1980S, ECONOMIC POLICYMAKERS made steady progress in reducing inflation. We have previously encountered inflation in its most insidious form: hyperinflation. Like post–World War I Germany, Hungary experienced a brutal bout of hyperinflation after World War II. At one point, annual inflation in Hungary reached 419,000,000,000,000,000 per cent, and the government issued a 100-quintillion note ('1' followed by twenty zeros).[1] In 1989, with prices doubling every month, Argentina's government announced that the country had exhausted its supply of banknote paper. It had literally run out of paper. Under Robert Mugabe, Zimbabwe's hyperinflation reached a point where prices were doubling every day. In one instance, Zimbabwean ATMs for a major bank gave a 'data overflow error' because they could not handle the number of zeros in the withdrawal.[2]

The risk of hyperinflation had spurred the adoption of the gold standard, which fixed a currency's value to the precious metal. In practice, this turned out to be clunky. There was no reason to expect the pace of world gold mining to match the rate of economic growth in countries that used the gold standard. If miners encounter a vast gold deposit, do we really want it to reduce the value of money? The end of the gold standard in the early 1970s meant that countries could increase the money supply in line with growth in the population and living standards. Major economies also began to decouple their currencies from one another, abandoning fixed exchange rates in favour of 'floating' exchange rates, which were set by the supply and demand for their currency.

But in the era when central banks were under the control of politicians, economic factors weren't the only consideration in managing inflation. Governments found it tempting to engineer a pre-election boom, which was often followed by a post-election bust. It might have helped politicians keep their jobs, but many regular workers lost their jobs in the crash that tended to follow the election. The problem is so stark that you can literally pick the election years out of the economic charts. In the post-war decades, economic growth rates in the United States tended to be lower in the year after the election than in the election year itself. A similar pattern could be seen in Europe.

Sometimes the political meddling in interest rate setting was direct, but it could also be covert. Facing rising inflation in 1972, US president Richard Nixon feared that the Federal Reserve would slow the economy by increasing interest rates. In an attempt to bully the central bank, Nixon leaked the falsehood that Federal Reserve Chair Arthur Burns was demanding a 50 per cent pay rise.[3]

The exposure of the 'political business cycle' led to a new development. Fiscal policy would still be controlled by elected politicians, but monetary policy would be carried out independently by central banks. Across the advanced world, the 1980s saw a steady increase in the degree of independence of central bankers. Step by step, central bankers in high-income nations moved from having no more autonomy than regular public servants towards having almost the kind of independence enjoyed by judges.

Not only were central bankers increasingly independent; they also began to target inflation directly. In the 1970s and 1980s, central banks had been targeting intermediate metrics – such as the quantity of money or credit – but there was an increasing recognition that the relationship between inflation and the money supply could be rubbery. As one frustrated central banker put it, 'We didn't abandon the monetary aggregates, they abandoned us.'[4]

Beginning in 1990, the New Zealand government required its central bank to keep inflation between 0 and 2 per cent, making it the first country to ask its central bank to explicitly focus on inflation. After many years of double-digit annual inflation, New Zealand sought an end to such wild price volatility.

Other countries swiftly followed. Canada in 1991. The United Kingdom in 1992. Australia in 1993. Today, most central banks have adopted inflation targets, typically around

2 per cent – a level that is thought to keep prices stable, while avoiding deflation. Just as high inflation can cause instability, deflation is a problem because it can stall spending, as households put off major purchases in anticipation of buying products more cheaply next year.

In practical terms, central banks control short-term interest rates. This allows them to affect the long-term interest rates charged by commercial banks for household and business borrowing.

Why does the interest rate have such a big effect on the economy? One way to think about interest rates is that they reflect the 'price' of choosing to consume today rather than tomorrow. When interest rates are low, businesses and individuals have an incentive to bring forward their plans. Want to open a new office or buy a house? Low interest rates might just tip the balance. Conversely, higher interest rates make borrowing less attractive, reducing economic activity by encouraging delayed gratification. To the central bank, interest rates are like the brake and accelerator on a car – tap the correct pedal at the right time, and you can promptly get to your destination without running off the road.

Some central banks target only inflation, while other central banks have a dual mandate, focusing on additional factors such as unemployment. In practice, this may be a smaller difference than it appears. Thanks to the work of Bill Phillips – the man who built a hydraulic model of the economy – we know that in the short term there is a strong relationship between inflation and unemployment. So a central bank that focuses on inflation will invariably affect jobs and growth too. The aim is to keep the economy in a 'goldilocks state' – not too cold, not too hot.

Have inflation targeting and central bank independence been a success? In terms of inflation, yes. Following the oil shocks of the 1970s, annual inflation in the United States was over 6 per cent for ten years, peaking at 14 per cent in 1980.[5] Through the 1990s and 2000s, inflation stayed low. It was a similar story in the UK and Japan, where inflation peaked at over 20 per cent in the 1970s, before being brought down to a low and steady level in the 1990s and 2000s.

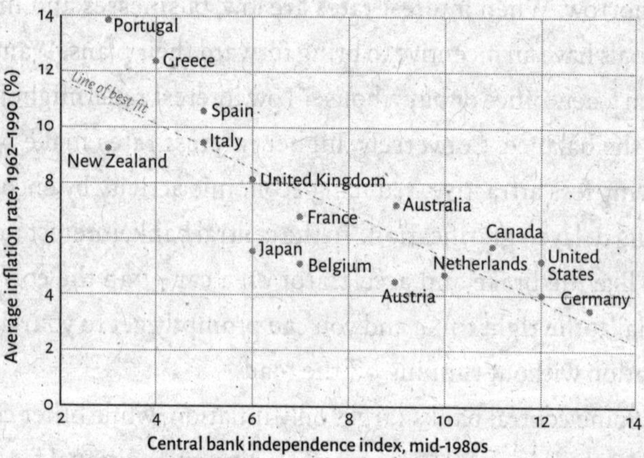

Inflation and central bank independence in advanced countries

The challenge for central bankers is that interest rates affect future behaviour, so monetary policy will always be shaped by their best guess of what is about to happen. As the head of the US Federal Reserve once put it, the aim is to take away the punch bowl just as the party is warming up.[6] As we will see, the early decades of the twenty-first century posed fresh challenges for central bankers as they tried to get the balance right.

While New Zealand was pioneering inflation targeting, India was preparing to implement some of the most significant reforms in its history – changes that went directly to the balance between government and the market. In 1991, Indian finance minister Manmohan Singh presented a budget to parliament that abolished most of the 'licence raj' – the system that dictated what firms could produce. The rupee was devalued, benefiting exporters, and some industries were opened to foreign investment. The spur for reform had been a crisis in foreign exchange. India had barely enough foreign currency to last a fortnight and had just shipped forty-seven tonnes of gold to London as collateral for an emergency loan.[7] The changes, Singh argued, would mark India's emergence as a 'major economic power in the world'.

Like Britain's repeal of the Corn Laws in 1846 and China's shift towards private property in 1978, India's 1991 reforms had a massive impact on the economy. Economic growth accelerated, and the private sector grew rapidly. The Tata Group, India's largest multinational conglomerate, expanded its operations in everything from chemical production to consulting services. In a neat reversal of colonialism, Tata purchased the United Kingdom's largest tea maker, Tetley, and iconic British car brand Jaguar. However, the story of the

Indian reforms is also a reminder of the risk of focusing on averages. In the pre-reform era, Indian incomes grew much more quickly for the bottom 50 per cent than for the top 1 per cent. In the post-reform period, Indian incomes grew substantially faster for the top 1 per cent than for the bottom 50 per cent.[8]

India is a more challenging environment for new entrepreneurs than many other low-income nations. In 2020, the World Bank estimated that starting a business in India requires ten procedures, takes seventeen days, and costs nearly one month's average earnings.[9] At the other extreme, starting a business in the Eastern European nation of Georgia requires one procedure, takes a day and costs the equivalent of one week's average wages.

For the second half of the twentieth century, trade volumes had grown faster than global economic output, reflecting increasing economic integration. But the trend accelerated from 1985 to 1995 – a period that one trade historian refers to as the decade in which 'the world changed'.[10] Some countries became more open because they had exhausted their supply of foreign exchange. Other nations were persuaded by global institutions such as the World Bank and the International Monetary Fund that trade would boost prosperity. The wave of democratisation that swept the world in this decade also tilted politics towards lower tariffs and away from protecting crony companies.

In 1994, the World Trade Organization finally came into being. Half a century earlier, Bretton Woods had envisaged the creation of an 'International Trade Organisation', but the US Senate had baulked at the proposal, forcing the world to rely instead on the General Agreement on Tariffs and Trade. Yet despite this clunky name, the institution oversaw a reduction in the average worldwide tariff from 22 per cent in 1947 to 3 per cent today.[11]

Another spur to trade was the decision by eleven high-income European countries to adopt a common currency, the Euro. Commencing in 1999, the Euro made it easier for people to trade and travel. The downside was that participating countries lost the flexibility to devalue their currency in a crisis. This danger was brought into sharp relief a decade later, when the European Debt Crisis caused a deep recession in Greece.

Trade was particularly important to the economic trajectory of Asian nations. Four 'tiger' economies (Korea, Taiwan, Hong Kong and Singapore) successfully adopted an export-led approach to economic growth, enjoying rapid gains in average incomes from the 1960s to the 1980s. In the 1980s, China negotiated most favoured nation agreements with the United States and the European Union, ensuring that tariffs on its exports would be no higher than those applying to other trading partners. In 2001, China joined the World Trade Organization.

Other Asian nations followed a similar path. In the 1990s, commentators began to talk about five 'tiger cub' economies – Indonesia, Malaysia, the Philippines, Thailand and Vietnam. An export-oriented manufacturing sector, foreign investment, and gains in education contributed to the rise of these countries from low-income to middle-income over the course of two generations. One way to see the effect is to compare these more open economies with the more closed economies of Latin America (such as Brazil and Argentina). In the middle of the twentieth century, East Asian living standards were less than half the level in Latin America. By the end of the century, the gap had almost closed.[12]

The shift of financial power towards Asia was highlighted when a Singapore options trader brought down Barings, the oldest merchant bank in London. Twenty-eight-year-old Nick Leeson was trading in derivatives – financial instruments that derive their value from another asset. The simplest derivatives are agricultural futures. Suppose a wheat farmer is worried about changes in the price of wheat between now and harvest day. The futures market allows her to sell her crop at today's price for delivery on a future day. Another form of derivative is an option to buy or sell at a given price, which can be used to shift risk.

But just as insurance shifts risk from the customer to the insurance company, derivatives involve shifting risk to another trader. Leeson's early trades for Barings had gone well, accounting in one year for a tenth of the firm's profits, but when he ran into problems, he set up an 'error account' to hide his losses from the management team. In 1995, Leeson placed a trade that amounted to a bet that the Japanese stock market would not fall. When the Kobe earthquake hit, he lost the bet. The problem was made worse by the dangers of derivative trading. When you own shares, the worst that can happen is that their value goes to zero. By contrast, when you own certain derivatives, your losses are unlimited. Barings lost more than US$1 billion. The bank collapsed and Leeson was jailed. A generation on, derivatives continue to be scrutinised by regulators. Derivatives can reduce risk for individual traders, yet they can also make the whole financial system more volatile.

Despite the volatility of financial markets, the story of the 1990s for many people in Asia was one of growing prosperity. Explaining economic development is a central goal of economics, and someone who has provided fresh insights into how poor countries become rich has one of the most unusual life stories of any economist.

At the age of twenty-six, Justin Yifu Lin was serving in the Taiwanese army as a company commander on Taiwan's Kinmen Island, a few kilometres from the Chinese mainland. He told his men that there would be a military exercise that night, and that if they saw anyone in the water they were not to shoot. Then, after dark, he entered the water and swam to the Chinese mainland, where he defected to the communist regime. The following year, studying economics at Peking University, he had another lucky break. Nobel Prize–winning economist Theodore Schultz was visiting China, and Lin served as his translator. Schultz was so impressed with the young man that he arranged a full scholarship for him to complete his PhD at Chicago University. A successful research career followed.

Lin's theory, expressed in numerous books, articles and speeches during his time as the World Bank's chief economist, is that the low-income countries which did best in the post-war era not only shared a market orientation, stable macroeconomic policies and an economic openness, but were also guided by a proactive state.[13] Governments in these countries identified business sectors that they saw as having a comparative advantage, and assisted them by establishing special economic zones, investing in infrastructure and promoting foreign investment. Where Raúl Prebisch's Latin American approach advised countries to wall themselves off from foreign competition, Lin's East Asian strategy suggested that countries support key export industries by funding research and building infrastructure. Yet even this approach is risky, since governments may pick the wrong sector, or find that a temporary policy has become permanent. As the critics note, 'infant industry' support often endures for industries that are well out of diapers.

Even in the most market-oriented nations, governments have played a powerful role in spurring technological development.[14] University College London's Mariana Mazzucato points out that major technological breakthroughs have often come when governments have invested in technological 'missions' – such as landing on the Moon or building the internet. The 'entrepreneurial state' has been a driving force behind innovations that are often wrongly attributed to the private sector.

The rapid spread of technology has been a key reason why world population and life expectancy have continued to rise. In 1798, cleric Thomas Malthus argued that the supply of food could not outpace population growth and a large-scale famine and population die-off was inevitable. In 1968, biologists

Anne and Paul Ehrlich declared that 'the battle to feed all of humanity is over'. They went on to forecast that 'in the 1970s the world will undergo famines – hundreds of millions of people are going to starve to death'. The Ehrlichs callously advised ending all food aid to India, a nation that was 'so far behind in the population-food game that there is no hope that our food aid will see them through to self-sufficiency'.

India's population is now more than twice as large as it was when the Ehrlichs wrote their book. Malnutrition and child mortality are down, while life expectancy and average heights are up. India's fertility rate has fallen below the 'replacement rate' of 2.1 births per woman – the level at which the population can be expected to sustain itself.[15] On current projections, the global fertility rate will fall below the replacement rate in approximately a generation, after which the world population will peak at around 10 billion people and then begin to decline.[16]

Why were Malthus and the Ehrlichs wrong? A major reason is that innovation debunked the doomsayers. Barbed wire allowed large animals to be contained cheaply, facilitating large-scale cattle and sheep farming. Tractors enabled larger-scale cropping, saving farmers vast numbers of hours of labour. The Haber-Bosch process made it possible to convert atmospheric nitrogen into ammonia-based fertiliser. Instead of mining tropical islands for guano, fertiliser is produced industrially, with global production exceeding two hundred million tonnes each year. Half the nitrogen in your body right now was created using the Haber-Bosch process.[17]

A key development in the 'green' revolution' of the 1960s was the breeding of semi-dwarf, disease-resistant wheat, which could produce nearly twice as much as regular wheat. Norman Borlaug, who led the introduction of these plants into India, Pakistan and Mexico, is credited with saving over one billion lives. More recently, genetically modified crops have allowed farmers to increase yields while reducing pesticide use. More than one-tenth of the world's cropland is now genetically modified. Declining usage of pesticides – partly spurred by Rachel Carson's book *Silent Spring* – has been good for the natural environment. It has also contributed to a drop in pesticide poisonings and farmer suicides.[18] Researchers are currently exploring a range of possible genetic modifications, including vitamin-augmented vegetables, and plants that carry out photosynthesis more efficiently.

In medicine, modern antibiotics transformed how doctors treat bacterial infections. A century ago, the son of US president Calvin Coolidge died from an infected blister on his toe after a game of tennis. A few years later, penicillin was discovered by Alexander Fleming. By the time of the D-Day landing, millions of doses of penicillin were ready for Allied troops. In the post-war era, penicillin was made available for civilian use. Today, antibiotics are used (and overused) across medicine and agriculture. Vaccines for tuberculosis, tetanus, polio, hepatitis B, measles, influenza, pneumonia and Covid have saved millions of lives.

Economists have also been instrumental in expanding the take-up of effective treatments. In the 1990s, experts disagreed on whether anti-malarial bed nets should be sold or freely given away. Some argued that villagers who received a free bed net would not value it as highly and might choose to use it as an inefficient fishing net, rather than a lifesaving protection for themselves and their children. To settle the matter, researchers conducted a series of large-scale randomised trials, in which some recipients were offered free bed nets, while others were given a chance to buy them at a subsidised price. It turned out that free bed nets had a much higher take-up rate and were equally likely to be used for their intended purpose.[19] As a result, donor agencies shifted towards the provision of free bed nets. Led by Esther Duflo, Abhijit Banerjee, Michael Kremer and Dean Karlan, randomised trials have become ubiquitous in development economics. The strength of randomisation is that it provides a powerful means of identifying causal effects.

It is easy to overlook the massive increase in global population and life expectancy that has been facilitated by health and agricultural innovation. Since 1800, the world's population has grown from 1 billion to 8 billion people. Back then, no country had an average life expectancy above forty years. Today, every nation has an average life expectancy above forty years. Global average life expectancy has risen from under thirty in 1800 to over seventy today.

From an economic standpoint, this increase in life expectancy may well be more important than the increase in average incomes. Suppose you could choose between living healthily for twice as long or having twice as much income – which would you pick? I'd go for the longevity, and I know many friends who would do the same. This point also serves as a reminder that what lies at the heart of economics is wellbeing, not income. As Australian-born economist Justin Wolfers notes, economics is no more about money than architecture is about inches. Money is a useful measuring tool when comparing costs and benefits, but it is not the ultimate end goal.

None of this is to suggest that technological progress and access to global markets have solved all the world's problems. Many nations appear to be stuck in a 'middle-income trap' – unable to make the leap into high-income status. Those countries that have accomplished this transition – such as Japan, Singapore and South Korea – are the exceptions. At the end of 2020, 719 million people were in extreme poverty – defined as living on less than US$2.15 a day. Most of those people live in Sub-Saharan Africa.

In most countries around the world, inequality has risen over the past generation. In some countries, the rich have not just accelerated away from the rest, but the poor have become poorer. Following the break-up of the Soviet Union, alcoholism increased, mortality rates rose and oligarchs thrived. The poorest half of Russians have real incomes about one-quarter below where they were in 1980.[20] Since the end of communism in 1989, 99 per cent of Russia's growth has gone to the top tenth of income earners. Putin's Russia is probably more unequal than the nation ruled by Tsar Nicholas II.

One way of visualising the distribution of global growth is what has come to be known as 'the elephant curve'. This chart, originally created by Serbian-born economist Branko

Milanović, and since updated by other researchers, depicts the growth rates experienced across the world's income distribution from 1980 to 2016: with the poorest people on the left, the richest on the right, and the global middle class in the centre.

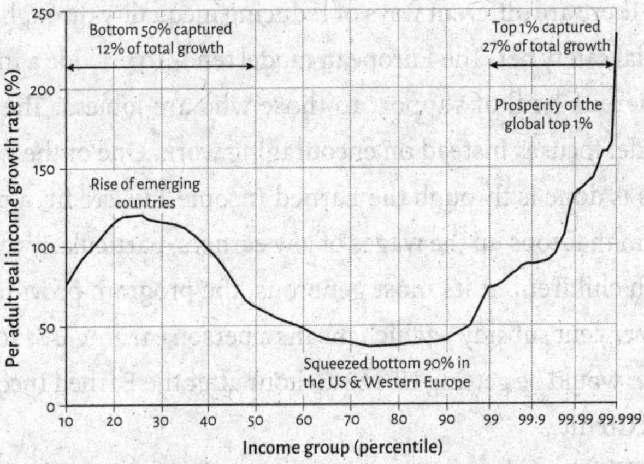

Total income growth by percentile across the world, 1980–2016

If you squint, you might make out the shape of an elephant: sluggish growth at the very bottom (the tail), more rapid growth for those between the twentieth and thirtieth percentiles (the back), then weak growth for the upper-middle (the downward curve of the trunk), and spectacular growth among the those with the highest incomes (the tip of the trunk). Strong economic growth in the emerging economies gives a pronounced hump. The squeezed middle in advanced nations traces the bottom of the trunk. And the rising prosperity of the global elite produces the upstretched trunk, pointing skywards.

In general, countries tend to be more equal if education keeps pace with technological developments, if unions are strong and if taxes are progressive. Equality is also improved if the economic growth rate (g) keeps pace with the rate of return on capital (r).

There are different ways of reducing inequality through the social safety net. The European model tends to provide a more generous level of support to those who are jobless. The US model focuses instead on encouraging work. One of the ways this is done is through the Earned Income Tax Credit, a program that tops up the wages of low earners, particularly those with children. At its most generous, the program provides a 40 per cent subsidy – which means a person earning US$20 an hour would be getting US$28 an hour after the Earned Income Tax Credit.

Which of the two models is better depends on what you think technology will do to the world of work.[21] The job pessimists argue that artificial intelligence–driven robots are steadily getting smarter and will soon be able to do every task imaginable – so we had better prepare for a workless world. The job optimists point out that this kind of argument has accompanied plenty of past waves of technology, from mechanical knitting machines to desktop computers, yet work is still around. As a congenital optimist, my own inclination is towards policies that encourage work. For many of us, a job isn't just a source of income, it's also a source of meaning and identity. People who lose their jobs experience a happiness drop that goes well beyond the loss of a pay packet.

It's too early to give up on the world of work.

Health care is another area where the US model differs markedly from the European model. One way to think about this is the 'iron triangle of health care', which posits that health systems face trade-offs between cost, quality and access.[22] The United States provides high-quality health care to those lucky enough to be covered, but spends more on health care than any other advanced nation, while still leaving some people uncovered. European systems are less likely to give patients the very latest treatments, but tend to be universal.

The economics of health care reminds us that some technological breakthroughs justify additional health spending.[23] Beta blockers have lowered the incidence of heart attacks, and the increased use of surgery to treat heart attacks has substantially increased the odds that a patient survives. For low-birth-weight infants, special ventilators and treatments such as artificial surfactants to improve lung development have raised the odds that a tiny baby will grow up healthy. Cataract surgery has gone from a substantial procedure that involved a three-night hospital stay and frequent complications to a day procedure that takes less than half an hour. Each of these technological developments has given us an increase in healthy life expectancy that justifies the investment. Yet in areas such as spinal fusion for back pain, there seems to be little evidence that patients are healthier. With the rise of personalised medicine and robotic surgery, the iron triangle of health care will be further tested. The choices countries make will affect both growth and inequality.

The most unequal countries have tended to underinvest in public services, a phenomenon that economist John Kenneth Galbraith once called 'private opulence and public squalor'.[24] In Rio de Janeiro, crime-stricken favelas can easily be seen from the luxury hotels that line Ipanema beach. In Cape Town, those who live in the city's mansions use private generators, private transport, private education and private security, while those in shacks must survive with intermittent power, unreliable trains, struggling schools and an annual murder rate of 1 in 1500. In Delhi, the most affluent families boast retinues of servants, while air pollution is among the worst in the world.

The wealth gap in Rio de Janeiro, with swimming pools next to shanty towns.

THE ECONOMICS OF SPORT

Sport constitutes less than 1 per cent of the global economy, but it can serve as a microcosm for understanding economic behaviour more broadly.[25] The discipline dates back to analysis of the baseball labour market in the 1950s, but it exploded around the turn of the millennium, marked by the formation of the *Journal of Sports Economics* in 2000.

Market structure matters. The problem of monopoly power is even greater in sport than in the regular economy. Few fans want to witness a walkover. To maintain 'competitive balance', many sporting codes share revenues, cap salaries and give bottom-of-the-league teams preference when drafting players for the next season.

Sport is a useful laboratory for studying how snap judgements can be racially biased, with a study of NBA basketball referees finding that they tend to give more personal fouls to players of the opposite race.[26] Sport also provided insights into the impact of long Covid. Studying European soccer players in the season before vaccines became available, those who had caught Covid noticeably underperformed. Even eight months after their infection, these young athletes made 5 per cent fewer passes than their Covid-free teammates.[27]

When teams are more evenly matched, crowd attendance is larger

Sport is an arena in which people respond to the incentives created by the rules – even if they are outside the spirit of the game.[28] In the 2012 Olympics, four teams in the women badminton doubles were disqualified for attempting to lose early matches so as to get a better draw in the knockout stages of the tournament. Incentives are everywhere.

12

HOT MARKETS AND A HOTTER PLANET

AT THE START OF 2000, the website pets.com ran a million-dollar Super Bowl ad, featuring its sock puppet mascot, and held an initial public offering, which raised US$82 million. By the end of the year, the stock price had crashed from US$11 a share to US$0.19 a share. It turned out that the company had a clever marketing strategy, but its business strategy was based on selling cat litter and dog food at prices well below cost. This meant that the more customers pets.com attracted, the more money it lost. Pets.com became the mascot for that year's tech wreck.

In the prior decade, the web had grown rapidly. This 'Web 1.0' phase saw the growth of search engines, file-sharing, government websites and commercial activity. By the end of the twentieth century, the number of worldwide internet users was doubling annually.[1] Some firms, such as Google and Amazon, would go on to dominate their industries. Others, like pets.com, eToys, GeoCities, Webvan and garden.com, could not produce enough revenue to satisfy their investors.

The bursting of the US technology bubble – like the Asian Financial Crisis a few years earlier – turned out to be a regional slump rather than a global one. From its peak in 2000, the tech-heavy NASDAQ share market fell by 78 per cent, and the September 2001 terrorist attacks prolonged the downturn. Yet the recession was relatively brief, and the rise in unemployment was relatively modest. Many nations, including the United Kingdom, Canada and Australia, avoided recession entirely.

In 2002, the Nobel Prize in economics was awarded to Princeton's Daniel Kahneman, for his work in developing behavioural economics. The economics prize was not one of the original Nobel Prizes; it only began in 1969, funded by the Swedish central bank to honour its 300th anniversary. Non-economists sometimes question whether it is a real Nobel Prize, but to economists, it is the profession's highest honour.

Kahneman is a psychologist, and his work shows a series of systematic departures from the standard rational model of *Homo economicus*. You are 8,000 times more likely to die from a mosquito bite than a shark bite, and 4,000 times more likely to die in a car crash than a plane crash.[2] But many people worry more about sharks and planes than mosquitoes and cars. We waste money on slot machines while under-saving for retirement. Restaurants make us spend more by putting an expensive item on the menu (it inflates our estimate of what a reasonable meal should cost). Online retailers trick us into unnecessary purchases through time-limited 'lightning deals'. Our night selves stay up late because – as comedian

Jerry Seinfeld once put it – getting only five hours of sleep is a problem for 'morning guy'.

Working with Amos Tversky (who would have shared the Nobel if he had not passed away in 1996), Kahneman's contribution was to take behavioural economics beyond a series of quirky results and incorporate it into an overall theory of decision-making. The brain, Kahneman argues, uses two 'systems'.[3] System One is fast, instinctive and emotional. This system is predisposed to behavioural biases. The anchoring bias means that people are more likely to buy a product if it has been marked down from an initially higher price. The planning fallacy means that the typical kitchen remodelling project ends up costing twice what was anticipated at the outset. System One is used when we are making snap judgements or applying rules of thumb, and tends to be prone to bias.

System Two is more rational, but slower. When multiplying 2 × 2, we use System One. When multiplying 17 × 24, we use System Two. System Two is more effortful and tends to be more rational. When deciding what kind of washing machine to buy, it is worth engaging System Two so as to make the best possible decision. The point of Kahneman's work is not to ask us to be calculating and rational about every decision, but to recognise when our behavioural biases might cause us to make costly mistakes. Today, behavioural economics is taught as a standard part of economics, and its implications are especially important when studying how people take risks and buy insurance, how we trade off the future against the present, and how we can be 'nudged' into making better decisions.

One of the biggest decisions facing humanity is how to handle global warming. In 2005, the British government commissioned economist Nicholas Stern to write a report on the economics of climate change. Delivered the following year, the Stern Review was to be one of the most significant economic reports on climate change ever written. Economists had long been familiar with the concept of an externality, thanks to the work of Cambridge's Arthur Pigou nearly a century earlier. Suppose a dirty factory is located next to a laundry and that when the factory is running it deposits soot on the laundry's sheets. This is an example of a market failure, because the factory does not pay for the cost it imposes on the laundry. The simplest answer is a ban on polluting factories in laundry districts (or the reverse). Alternatively, the government could impose a 'Pigouvian tax', with the size of the tax equating to the value of the harm that the factory does to the laundry. Another economist, Ronald Coase, suggested that if transaction costs were sufficiently small, then the parties could bargain their way to an efficient outcome (though he acknowledged that this would rarely occur in practice).

In his report, Nicholas Stern concluded that climate change was the biggest market failure the world had ever seen. Carbon pollution imposed massive social costs, but emitters had faced little incentive to cut back. Left unchecked, Stern argued, climate change would have adverse impacts on food production, access to water, and population health. Water shortages, coastal flooding and hunger could affect hundreds of millions of people, disrupting life on a scale equivalent to the world wars. These costs would likely be equivalent to losing 5 per cent of global income every year forever – and might be as high as losing 20 per cent of global income each year. The Stern Review concluded that by spending a much smaller amount – approximately 1 per cent of global income – greenhouse emissions could be substantially reduced, limiting the worst impacts of climate change. The key to action was to ensure that investment which would inevitably be made – in modernising energy production, updating transport networks and so on – was done in a way that reduced carbon emissions.

Scientific reports from the Intergovernmental Panel on Climate Change had drawn the world's attention to the issue, with some scientists arguing that the planet had entered a new geological epoch, the Anthropocene. The Stern Review applied an economic lens: showing that the benefits of acting outweighed the costs. Central to the report's conclusion was that it put pretty much the same weight on the future as the present, choosing not to apply a normal economic discount rate to the future. This is different to how economists often analyse long-term decisions. In considering whether to build a motorway, a government will typically scale down future benefits to reflect the fact that the money could otherwise be invested, earning a return that would make it more valuable in the future.

With climate change, the analysis is different. If we use standard economic discount rates to diminish future costs, we are effectively saying that the lives of future generations should be considered less valuable than those of people living today. When assessing infrastructure projects, the US Office of Management and Budget suggests that agencies conduct their analysis using discount rates of up to 7 per cent. But a discount rate of 7 per cent implies that if benefits are a decade away, then they need to be twice as big as the costs, and that if they are a century away, they need to be 868 times the cost. Applied across individuals, this suggests that the value of one person living a century ago is equivalent to the value of 868 people living today. But would we really think that the value of King George V equates to the population of an entire high school today? To avoid such an absurd result, Stern opted to use a lower discount rate, placing increased weight on the wellbeing of future generations.

While the release of the Stern Review prompted debate among economists around the choice of discount rates, its essential conclusions are now broadly accepted. Economists have worked with governments to design a variety of schemes to reduce emissions – which are now falling in most advanced nations. A central challenge is China's greenhouse emissions, which account for one-third of the global total and have been steadily rising over recent years. Encouraging more low-income nations to reduce emissions is now central to addressing the world's biggest market failure.

Markets don't always fail, however, and it can be useful to recognise the amount of value created by the simple act of trading. Your morning cup of coffee likely costs less than the maximum you would be willing to pay: we call the difference 'consumer surplus'. Likewise, the café likely sells it for more than the minimum it would be willing to accept: we call that gap 'producer surplus'.

In 2005, Canadian blogger Kyle MacDonald vividly illustrated this principle by trading his way from a red paperclip to a house. First, he traded his paperclip for a fish-shaped pen. Then he traded the pen for a hand-sculpted doorknob. Then he traded the doorknob for a camp stove. This went on until his fourteenth and final trade: swapping a movie role for a small house. At each step, MacDonald valued the new item more highly than the old item – but he traded with someone who valued the old item more than the new. MacDonald didn't just get himself a house – he did so through fourteen trades that each made another person better off.

Kyle MacDonald with the first and last of his traded items.

MacDonald wasn't the only one who was keen to get his hands on a house. By 2005, the US economy had recovered from the short-lived tech crisis, and a housing boom was underway. This was an era when home prices were rising across the advanced world. On average, it took a middle-income couple with two children seven years of income in 1995 to pay for a 60 square metre (650 square foot) apartment in their country's capital city. By 2005, the price of that same apartment had risen to ten years of income.[4]

In the United States, the rise in prices was especially steep. In 2007, economist Robert Shiller took his series of US house prices over the previous century and plotted them on a rollercoaster simulation.[5] The simulator swooped viewers up and down, before finally taking them on a huge rise. As it ended, viewers could see that the rollercoaster was poised higher than ever before.

While prices were rising, lending standards were falling. In Bakersfield, California, a strawberry picker with an income of US$14,000 and no knowledge of English was lent the full purchase price of a US$720,000 home.[6] These NINJA loans (no income, no job, no assets) were written on the assumption that prices would continue to rise, allowing borrowers to refinance. On the lending side, loans were 'securitised' – which meant that they were packaged and sold on to investors. The theory was that this would distribute the risk more broadly and allow the market to grow more rapidly. The problem was that it changed the incentives. Traditionally, banks lent money to people to buy homes, and the bank lost money if the borrower couldn't repay. With securitisation, the people writing the loans were no longer taking the risk, which created an incentive to lend too much to people who could not afford to repay.

MIND THE GENDER PAY GAP

Worldwide, hourly wages for women are 20 per cent less than for men.[7] This represents a sizeable gap, though it has narrowed over time. On average, the gender pay gap was twice as large in the 1960s as it is today.[8] In Europe from 1300 to 1800, the gender pay gap was larger still, with women often earning only half as much as men.[9]

What explains the gender pay gap? Historically, one factor was that women had less formal education than men. That's no longer true, with women's educational attainment exceeding men's in most countries. But a significant factor is the occupations that men and women work in. Jobs in the care economy are dominated by women and tend to pay lower wages. Occupations such as engineering and computer programming are male-dominated and tend to pay above-average wages.

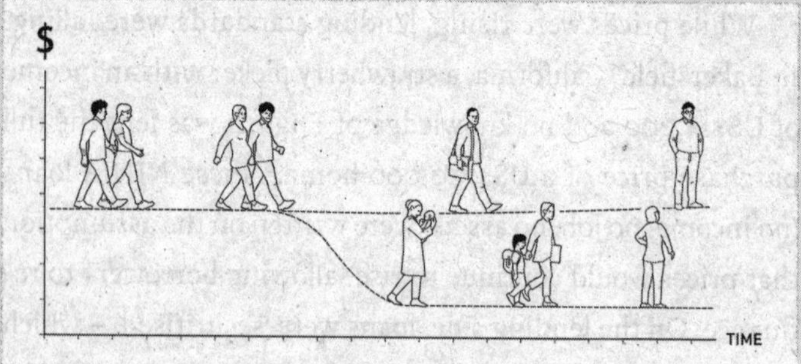

Claudia Goldin won the 2023 Nobel Memorial Prize in Economic Sciences 'for having advanced our understanding of women's labour market outcomes'. To accompany its announcement, the Royal Swedish Academy of Sciences released this cartoon, illustrating Goldin's findings on the role of parenthood in widening the gender pay gap.

In the past, some economists thought that men and women were freely choosing their occupations. Recent research has questioned this view. For example, we know that women are more likely to be sexually harassed at work, and that this harassment can deter women from certain occupations.

If technical jobs have higher rates of sexual harassment, then this can widen the gender pay gap by discouraging women from choosing those career pathways.

Another factor is discrimination. Women report higher levels of discrimination at work, although this has diminished over the past century. One intriguing study following transgender men and women finds that those who transition female tend to experience a wage drop, while those who transition male tend to experience a wage gain.[10]

Perhaps the largest contributor to the gender pay gap in the modern era is the motherhood penalty. In many nations, earnings trajectories for childless men and women are not dramatically different. But among those who have children, women generally spend more time out of the labour force than men. When women have children, their earnings typically fall or flatline. This is not only because mothers often work part time, but also because they can find themselves on a less attractive career trajectory, sometimes dubbed 'the mummy track'. With less experience in the labour market, women are paid lower wages than men.

This pay gap is particularly large in what Harvard economist Claudia Goldin calls 'greedy jobs'.[11] In many countries, women are severely underrepresented in time-intensive roles such as chief executives, law firm partners, politicians and surgeons. Occupations that make it difficult to combine career and family tend to have the highest gender pay gaps. Likewise, gender gaps are larger in countries where access to childcare is more limited. One consequence of the motherhood penalty is that the gender pay gap tends to be much bigger if we measure it in terms of lifetime earnings rather than hourly wages. Even in advanced countries, the average lifetime earnings of mothers are only about half the lifetime earnings of men – similar to the hourly wage gap five hundred years ago.[12]

Investment bank Goldman Sachs was one of the financial organisations that bundled together risky 'subprime' housing loans into mortgage-backed securities. Buyers of these securities effectively owned a slice of many mortgages. That reduced investors' exposure if a single NINJA homeowner defaulted on their loan, but still left investors vulnerable if the whole housing market slumped. Goldman marketed these products widely, including to retirement funds. One Goldman trader boasted of selling subprime mortgages to 'widows and orphans'. Meanwhile, Goldman was betting that the housing market would fall – a trade that became known as 'the big short'. Goldman would later argue that it had made no secret of the fact that it was betting against the product it was selling to its customers.

When the market crashed, average US home values dropped by around one-fifth. By 2008, one in ten mortgage holders had negative equity – meaning that their mortgage was worth more than their home. Millions of borrowers defaulted on their loans and lost their homes. Yet Goldman Sachs emerged financially unscathed. In 2009, the firm made a profit of US$13 billion, and paid billions of dollars in bonuses. Goldman's chief executive, Lloyd Blankfein, received a US$9 million bonus.

The financial crisis has been compared with Agatha Christie's *Murder on the Orient Express*, in which everybody did it. Greedy bankers, incompetent credit rating agencies, gullible home owners and lax policymakers each bear some share of the blame. In response, coordinated action by the G20 delivered fiscal stimulus across the world's twenty largest economies. But many still suffered enduring harm. In the US, the unemployment rate for Black workers rose above 10 per cent, and stayed there for more than six years, while the unemployment rate among white workers never reached double digits.[13] This is a common pattern in recessions across countries. Education and assets serve as shock absorbers – making people less vulnerable to crises. Conversely, economists are realising that volatility and disadvantage go together.

Development economists have increasingly pinpointed the role of corruption in holding economies back. In 2009, Malaysian prime minister Najib Razak established a sovereign wealth fund known as 1MDB, which was used to channel hundreds of millions of dollars of public money into political campaigns for his party, and personal spending for his associates. Jho Low, a key mastermind of the scam, purchased multimillion-dollar homes in London, New York and Los Angeles, a US$35 million Bombardier Global 5000 jet, US$8 million of jewellery for his then-girlfriend Miranda Kerr, and a multi-day party that involved chartering an international flight to celebrate New Year's Eve in both Sydney and Las Vegas. The stolen money was even used to fund *The Wolf of Wall Street* – a film about a fraudulent stockbroker and his opulent lifestyle. At one point, Low was thought to have more free cash at his disposal than anyone else in the world.

Economists studying corruption have noted the various ways that it can stymie development. The thefts perpetrated by Indonesia's president Suharto, Zaire's president Mobutu and the Philippines' president Marcos reduced growth and increased inequality in their countries. Public money stolen to buy palaces, luxury cars and yachts is not available to be spent on government health and education programs. In business, corruption raises prices, lowers innovation and undermines honest public servants. Corruption flourishes when economic power meets crooked politics outside the public eye. One researcher sums up the drivers of corruption in an equation: corruption equals monopoly plus discretion minus accountability.[14]

Economists are also increasingly recognising the role of tax havens in enabling corruption. The 1MDB embezzlement was enabled by bank accounts in the British Virgin Islands. The Panama Papers, Pandora Papers, Lux Leaks and other disclosures have revealed widespread use of tax havens by drug lords, dictators and money launderers, as well as by the ultra-wealthy. On one estimate, four out of every five dollars in offshore accounts is there in breach of other countries' tax laws.[15] Economic research on the scale of the problem has helped put pressure on tax havens to share information with tax administrations around the world.

In low-income countries, the program Tax Inspectors Without Borders provides expertise to enable nations to conduct rigorous audits – in some cases producing tax gains 100 times larger than the cost of paying the auditors. Another useful approach is the concept of 'odious debt', under which the international community agrees that money lent to a despot is not a true loan to the government but should be regarded as a personal loan.[16] The idea of odious debt is to change lenders' incentives. If a bank knows that a loan to help an autocrat buy weapons will be void if the country becomes a democracy, then it might think twice before making the loan in the first place. In turn, this may help to defund dictators.

As growth resumed after the financial crisis, so too did the steady realisation that some of the claims made by the world's money managers might be hollow. In one exercise, researchers followed up the forty-three companies profiled in Tom Peters and Robert Waterman's book *In Search of Excellence*. They found that just two years later, almost one-third were in serious financial trouble.[17] The most influential business book of its era didn't always identify the most successful firms. In another exercise, Raven, a six-year-old chimpanzee, outperformed 99 per cent of professional Wall Street brokers by throwing darts to choose her stocks.[18]

The big question for fund managers is whether they can beat the average performance of the share market. According to a recent report, 65 per cent of actively managed US equity funds underperform the share market over a one-year period.[19] In other words, the typical year sees about two-thirds of actively managed funds grow by less than the share market average. Over a five-year period, the share of underperformers grows to 88 per cent. Over a ten-year period, 92 per cent of managed funds underperform the share market.

The problem isn't that these money-managers are stupid, it's that beating the share market is difficult, as economic theory predicts. When deciding whether to buy or sell a stock, analysts scrutinise every skerrick of information to understand the product, the management team and the market conditions. Share market analysts have been known to use satellite images to count cars in parking lots to estimate retail demand and to study long-range weather forecasts to predict crop yields. Algorithmic trading models are programmed to spot small pricing differences across markets and exploit the difference within milliseconds.

A basic maxim of the share market is the efficient market hypothesis: that the price of a stock reflects all publicly available information. Since it is illegal to trade based on 'insider' information, most actively managed funds – as well as most individual day traders – fail to beat the average return on the share market. As economists like to say, it's rare to find a $20 note on the sidewalk, because someone else is likely to have grabbed it first.

A popular alternative to actively managed funds is an index fund. An index fund simply comprises the companies on the share market, held in proportion to their market size. For example, an S&P 500 index fund today would include about 7 per cent Apple, 1 per cent Chevron, 0.1 per cent FedEx, and a proportionate share of the other 497 firms in the index. The returns on an index fund are designed to match the share index that it is tracking, minus a management fee. Because tracking the index is a trivial exercise, index funds can charge fees that are far smaller than actively managed funds that are paying stock pickers to choose their investments.

When Vanguard founder Jack Bogle created the index fund

in 1975, critics derided it as 'Bogle's folly'. But by the 2010s, index funds were the gorillas in the room. According to one estimate, these passive investors controlled one-fifth of the US share market in 2011 (a figure that would grow to two-fifths over the coming decade).[20] One of the big three index investors – Vanguard, BlackRock and State Street – is the largest shareholder for nine-tenths of the firms on the S&P 500.[21]

Economists quarrel about many things, but a survey of over forty top economists (including several Nobel Prize winners) found not a single economist who disagreed with the proposition that investors do better from investing in index funds.[22] Index funds even have the unlikely backing of Warren Buffett, who despite being an active investor believes that most people would be better off putting their money into low-cost index funds. 'If a statue is ever erected to honour the person who has done the most for American investors', Buffett wrote to his shareholders in 2017, 'the hands-down choice should be Jack Bogle.'

Across the world, the 2010s saw an unprecedented volume of money looking for investment opportunities. From Canadian pension funds to high-saving Chinese families, a global glut of savings began to push down interest rates. Harvard's Larry Summers warned that the world may be entering a period of 'secular stagnation', in which productivity and growth had slowed. George Mason University's Tyler Cowen argued that compared to the transformative twentieth-century breakthroughs of mass education, mass migration, electrification and transport, the economic gains from computerisation and smartphones were relatively modest.[23] Internet innovations such as Wikipedia, YouTube and Google had advantaged the intellectually curious, but had only a limited impact on productivity. A more optimistic view is that the productivity impacts of computing power – like coal power and electricity before it – could come decades after the innovation first emerged.

Low interest rates posed a challenge to monetary policymakers. Analysing historical data going back 5000 years, Bank of England economist Andy Haldane concluded that interest rates had never before been this low.[24] He likened central banks' attempts to raise interest rates to the story of a child whose kite gets lodged in a tree and who throws one thing after another into the branches in his attempts to dislodge it. Asset purchases, liquidity schemes and forward guidance, Haldane noted, had been similarly ineffective at raising interest rates. By the late 2010s, central bankers in many countries found themselves grappling with deflation.

A common problem for central bankers in this era was the 'zero lower bound' – arising from the fact that it's tricky to charge someone a negative rate of interest. If I can store cash without cost, why should I lend it to you so you can give me back less money than I started with? Central bankers turned instead to 'quantitative easing', purchasing financial assets in an attempt to support the economy. By the end of the 2010s, four major central banks – the US Federal Reserve, the Bank of England, the Bank of Japan and the European Central Bank – collectively held more than US$20 trillion in financial assets –

a sum approximately equal to the annual economic output of the United States.[25]

Some economic damage during this era was self-inflicted. After championing global efforts to reduce trade barriers for more than half a century, the United States abruptly reversed course in 2018, imposing tariffs on steel, aluminium and a plethora of imports from China. Announcing the tariffs, President Donald Trump characterised them as a way of punishing foreigners, but in fact the cost was largely borne by Americans. For US households, Trump's tariffs constituted one of the largest tax increases in decades.[26] Because many more US workers are employed in steel-using sectors such as construction and car manufacturing than in steel manufacturing, it has been estimated that sixteen jobs were lost for every additional job created.[27] Furthermore, trading partners imposed retaliatory tariffs, reducing US export volumes by 10 per cent for the affected products.[28] Like military wars, trade wars tend to produce more losers than winners.

In a 2016 referendum, 52 per cent of Britons voted to leave the European Union, which took effect in 2020. Brexit led many UK-based firms to shift offices to continental Europe and created considerable uncertainty for importers and exporters. Brexit impeded the free flow of people, services, goods and capital between the United Kingdom and continental Europe. The UK's Office of Budget Responsibility puts the long-run cost of Brexit at 4 per cent of UK income.[29] Economists were almost universal in opposing Brexit, but were unable to counter a campaign driven by anti-establishment sentiments, a backlash against immigration and a distrust of international institutions.

In the twenty-first century, economists turned our attention to a wide range of topics – from corruption to climate change – that might have been considered beyond the remit of the discipline in prior generations. Economists acknowledged the limitations of the purely rational model, using behavioural economics to explain why people often save too little and eat too much. And, like the debate over the Corn Laws and the *Smoot-Hawley Tariff Act*, the Trump tariffs and Brexit were a reminder that while openness may be good economics, isolationism often wins elections.

13

THE PANDEMIC AND BEYOND

IN EARLY 2020, THE EMERGENCE of Covid plunged the world economy into the worst downturn since the Great Depression of the 1930s. As countries locked down, global income in the second quarter of 2020 fell by 5 per cent.[1] Business investment plummeted, tourism and migration virtually ceased, and spending on services plunged. Every advanced economy entered recession. Across the world, around 400 million jobs were lost.[2] To support households, governments provided more than US$10 trillion in support to affected workers and firms. In 2019, global government debt was equivalent to ten months of worldwide income. In 2020, global government debt jumped to a full year of worldwide income.[3]

Two inventions were crucial. Covid tests helped solve what economists refer to as an 'information problem' – making it possible for people to self-isolate in the early phase of the disease so as not to infect others. Covid vaccines provided a substantial benefit to those taking them – reducing the chance of death to less than one-tenth of the risk for unvaccinated people.[4] Vaccines also provided a significant positive externality, by reducing the rate of disease spread. Because of this positive externality, governments around the world provided vaccines free, rather than asking people to pay for them.

To monetary policymakers, a surprise of Covid was the impact on inflation as lockdowns were lifted. Households unleashed a flood of pent-up spending, while Russia's invasion of Ukraine caused energy prices to spike. Suddenly central banks found themselves dealing with inflation that rivalled that of the 1970s. Because curbing inflation called for interest rate rises rather than reductions, there was no need for unconventional monetary policy. The problem was the anguish that high rates caused to mortgage holders and business owners who had become accustomed to cheap money. Many people questioned why central banks hadn't acted earlier, and why their forecasts had wrongly anticipated low inflation and low interest rates.

The answer goes to a general challenge in economics: forecasting is hard. Like weather forecasters and sports pundits, central bankers can't always be sure what's around the corner. As baseball philosopher Yogi Berra once put it, 'It's tough to make predictions, especially about the future.' Academic economists tend to be dubious of forecasts, noting that crises are often precipitated by unexpected shocks. Conflict, pandemics, famines, bankruptcies, defaults and trade wars are often missed by economic models that concentrate only on slow-moving variables.

As well as being attacked for having imperfect foresight,

central bankers have been criticised for a multitude of other sins. Why didn't they do more to prevent the build-up of government debt? Why did central banks in places like Australia, Ireland and the United States allow house prices to double within a decade around the start of the millennium? Why did central banks allow households to take on so much debt?

The answer is something known as the 'Tinbergen Rule', which simply notes that if you have only one tool, you can only target one objective. The primary tool for central banks is interest rates. The Tinbergen Rule points out that if house prices are skyrocketing while inflation is below the target, central banks can't solve both problems. Similarly, if families are facing runaway inflation, yet some households are overstretched on their mortgages, central banks must choose which problem to solve.

One contributing factor to supply chain blockages during the Covid pandemic was the high degree of concentration across many markets. In the United States, virtually all infant formula is made by a handful of companies, and imports are heavily restricted. When the largest manufacturer, Abbott, closed its biggest plant due to possible contamination, it caused a crisis. At its peak, seven out of ten US supermarkets carried no infant formula. The small number of producers had created chokepoints, and parents were paying the price.

The 'Chicago School' view of competition policy – that monopolies could serve consumers well in many instances – was coming under increasing scrutiny. From infant formula (where nine-tenths is made by four companies) to coffins (where the top two producers make four-fifths of all coffins), concentrated markets were literally a cradle-to-grave phenomenon.

Market concentration wasn't just the result of large firms outgrowing their competitors. Applying the Chicago School's consumer welfare standard, competition authorities and courts had allowed a plethora of mergers, including Facebook's purchase of Instagram, Google's purchase of YouTube, and brewer AB InBev's purchase of SABMiller. Yet economists were now concerned that market concentration might have other adverse impacts. In terms of annual income, the largest firms are on the scale of nations. Walmart is about the economic size of Thailand. Amazon is the size of Austria. ExxonMobil is the size of Peru. Perhaps, economists began to think, big wasn't beautiful after all.

The fear about market dominance was felt most keenly in technology, where a winner-takes-all dynamic often applies. In advanced nations, five firms known colloquially as 'MAMAA' – Meta, Apple, Microsoft, Alphabet and Amazon – dominate social media, smartphones, software, search and online shopping. In China, the four players known as 'BATX' – Baidu, Alibaba, Tencent and Xiaomi – dominate search, e-commerce, social media and smartphones.

Economists became increasingly concerned that concentrated markets hurt workers as well as consumers. One-fifth of US workers have a clause in their employment contract limiting their ability to take a job with any company that competes with their current employer.[5] A clandestine set of deals between Silicon Valley firms not to hire each other's software engineers reduced employees' salaries. Joan Robinson's concern about monopsony power remains highly relevant.

Monopsony power can also hurt suppliers. Apple's App Store has been described as a 'walled garden', in which Apple charges app developers up to 30 per cent of any revenue that they make through the app store. Similar concerns were being raised in China, where Alibaba was caught preventing merchants selling their goods on rival platforms, and fined the equivalent of US$2.8 billion. The nine firms – MAMAA and BATX – are among the world leaders in artificial intelligence. So they stand to gain dramatically from breakthroughs in computing technology.[6]

While many fear that technology may supersize the megacorps, technological advances could reduce the size of some companies. Ronald Coase's seminal analysis of the boundaries of the firm proposed that whether a job should be done in-house or outsourced depends on transaction costs and information costs. If online platforms make it easier to tap non-employees or connect with other organisations, they could end up shrinking the firm. Most Meta content moderators don't work for Meta. Most Amazon delivery drivers don't work for Amazon. In the future, multifaceted corporate conglomerates such as Mitsui, Swire and Tata may struggle against more specialised competitors.

Competition policy isn't the only area that is being affected by the increasing power and usage of computing technology. Mathematics professor Hannah Fry gives a series of examples in which algorithms have produced troubling results.[7] When they googled their own names, African Americans were more likely than white Americans to see advertisements targeted at people with criminal records. Women were less likely than men to be served online advertisements for high-paying executive jobs.

In one incident, the British supermarket Tesco was contacted by a customer who shared a store loyalty card with her husband and had seen condoms in the 'my favourites' section. It must be a mistake, she told the supermarket. It wasn't, but the supermarket quietly apologised for the data error, rather than be the cause of a marital rift. In the US justice system, judges sometimes make decisions based on algorithms that calculate the chances that a person will reoffend.[8] Yet defendants can be refused access to the information that has led to the decision. In China, the social credit system has denied millions of citizens access to flights and high-speed rail trips on the basis of their low 'trustworthiness', which can be due to jaywalking, failing to visit one's elderly parents, or criticising the government online.

Social psychologist Shoshana Zuboff dubs the use of private data by corporations 'surveillance capitalism', noting the way that it is leading to increasingly targeted advertising and a growing corporate demand for user data.[9] As the examples above show, big data has the potential to worsen inequality. Yet economists are also making use of large datasets to answer questions that were previously out of reach. One exemplar is Harvard's Raj Chetty, whose Opportunity Insights laboratory uses big data to study economic opportunity.

Using tax data on almost the entire US population over nearly three decades, Chetty's team analysed economic mobility – the propensity of people to move up or down the income distribution from one generation to the next.[10] For children born in the 1940s, they showed, nearly nine in ten could expect to earn more than their parents. But for children born in the 1980s, only half could expect to earn more than their parents. The research showed that neighbourhoods have a powerful causal impact on children. Mapping opportunity across the United States, they reported that counties with less concentrated poverty, less income inequality, better schools, a larger share of two-parent families, and lower crime rates generally produce better outcomes for children in poor families.

In another set of studies, analysing Facebook data for more than 70 million US residents, Chetty and his team showed that friendship networks are strongly class-based.[11] People in the top tenth of the socioeconomic distribution have twice as many friends who are also in the top tenth than they have friends in the bottom half of the distribution. The rich and poor also have different kinds of friends. Those at the top are more likely to have friends from university, while those at the bottom are more likely to have close friends in their neighbourhood. The researchers are also able to calculate friendship patterns at a local level – demonstrating that people in the US Midwest are more likely to be friends with people in a different social class.

FORENSIC ECONOMICS

Forensic economics has uncovered wrongdoing in surprising places.[12] One study compares snow reports from ski resorts with those from government weather stations. Ski resorts report more snowfall, and the gap is much larger on weekends. Another study finds that *Wine Spectator* magazine provides higher ratings – relative to other publications – to wines that advertise in its pages. Similarly, personal finance magazines are more likely to recommend the funds of their advertisers. Fashion magazines are more inclined to feature the outfits of their advertisers.

In figure skating, forensic economics finds that judges tend to give higher scores to athletes from their countries.

Incentives can distort behaviour. Observing what happens when real estate agents sell their own houses, an economic study reveals that agents' homes stay on the market for ten days longer and sell for 4 per cent more than average. Education economists find that on days when schools have high-stakes tests, they are more likely to suspend poorly performing pupils. Schools also serve higher-calorie foods on test days.

Forensic economics can even unearth corruption. When Indonesian dictator Suharto suffered health scares, the share price of politically connected firms dropped too. When conflicts worsen in countries that are under a United Nations arms embargo, stock prices of arms manufacturers rise. Drawing on work in psychology, researchers noted that humans have a bias in making up numbers. We overuse certain digits (such as 7) and consecutive pairs (such as 1–2 or 3–4). Election results from Nigeria and Iran show these suspicious patterns. Results from elections in Sweden and the United States do not. The richer the data, the more that forensic economics will reveal about poor behaviour.

Chetty's work is an example of the way in which economics has become more data-focused. In economics journals, it is increasingly rare to see research that sets out a theoretical model without using data to test its predictions. Economists' use of randomised experiments has grown massively since the preschool studies of the 1960s, and researchers have become more adept at using natural experiments to identify causal impacts. The rise in computing power has reduced the cost of analysing huge datasets. My own PhD research in 2004, analysing a dataset of more than one million people, could not have been done on a laptop a decade earlier.[13] A decade later, the code would have run in seconds rather than hours. Big data analytics is a beneficiary of Moore's Law.

Big data is also producing insights on uncomfortable topics such as sex and race. Crunching results from internet searches, Seth Stephens-Davidowitz found that in places that are least tolerant of homosexuality, people are more likely to google the question 'Is my husband gay?'[14] Searches for racist jokes correlate strongly with voting patterns for Donald Trump in the 2016 election. Parents are twice as likely to search for 'Is my son gifted?' than 'Is my daughter gifted?'. Parents are also twice as likely to search for 'Is my daughter overweight?' than 'Is my son overweight?' To reduce racism, sexism and homophobia, it is first vital to understand the problem. Big data makes it possible to go where surveys cannot.

Satellite data is also uncovering the truth about economic prosperity. At night, affluent parts of the world light up like a Christmas tree, while the poorest regions go dark.

A similar pattern holds within the same country over time: faster growth is associated with more light at night. Within the US, satellite data reveals the legacy of historical transport patterns. Back when many goods were moved by river, there were certain locations in the US that required portage between two boats. More than a century after portage ceased, these places continue to be thriving economic centres.[15] Another study, analysing global satellite data over two decades, found that dictators are more likely to lie about their country's growth – reporting better economic numbers than their satellite images would suggest.[16] Satellite images are also being used by researchers to study deforestation in Brazil and pollution in Indonesia. The images are now sufficiently fine-grained that they have allowed researchers to count the number of trees owned by individual farmers in Uganda, and to measure which houses in a Nairobi slum have upgraded their roofs.[17]

New kinds of data also remind us of the importance of updating economic statistics so that they measure what we care about. National income accounts were developed at a time when most jobs were on farms or in factories. The online economy poses new challenges to the bean-counters. In one study, people were asked how much they would have to be paid to give up various free internet services for a year.[18] People responded that they would have to be paid US$17,000 to give up search, US$8000 to forego email, US$3000 to lose maps, and US$1000 to sacrifice streaming video. Because national accounts measure value-added, not consumer well-being, they may miss these important benefits.

Unpaid work has been badly neglected in economic statistics. If a man pays a housekeeper to cook his dinner, clean his home and care for his child, then her income is included in the national accounts and she is regarded as part of the labour force. If they marry and she continues this work, then she no longer receives a wage (any money that moves between them is regarded as a transfer within the household), and she is counted as being outside the labour force.[19] Feminist economists have pointed out that unpaid work may account for most of the world's work. While researchers such as Auckland University of Technology's Marilyn Waring have cogently critiqued the way that economic statistics are collected, it remains the case that national income accounts include the work of men who manufacture handguns but exclude the work of women who breastfeed babies.[20] Using smartphones to better capture how people use their time, while maintaining user privacy, is a key frontier in modernising our economic statistics.

14

ECONOMICS: PAST, PRESENT AND FUTURE

ECONOMIST MAX ROSER ONCE OBSERVED that news frequency shapes news coverage.[1] Weekly magazines have a different focus from daily papers, which in turn have a different focus from social media. But what if we had a newspaper that came out every fifty years? Roser argued that such a newspaper would be far more likely to discuss long-term positive trends. Instead of celebrity gossip, the front page of a fifty-year newspaper today might report on the global child mortality rate dropping from 14 per cent to 4 per cent, or the fact that services employment now constitutes a majority of all jobs worldwide.[2]

This book began with the story of light – an example of how technology has turned something that was a luxury for our ancestors to something that is so trivially cheap that we rarely think about its cost. In the long sweep, much of economic development is like this. Advances in child health are epitomised by the story of Queen Anne – the most powerful woman of her age. Between 1684 and 1700, she fell pregnant seventeen times. All but one of her pregnancies ended in stillbirth, miscarriage or childhood death. Three centuries on, even the poorest parents are unlikely to lose a child. Advances in sanitation and medicine have saved millions of lives. In real terms, workers in most countries now earn more in a day than their counterparts of 1900 earned in a week.

From the plough to the internet, technology has driven revolutions in economic activity. Societies have also benefited from comparative advantage. Across the labour market, specialisation has played a vital role in increasing prosperity. If you've honed a set of skills, you'll know instinctively why a society of specialists can enjoy higher living standards than a group of generalists. And this principle plays out across countries as it does among individuals. Trade allows countries to specialise in what they do best. Having a trading partner isn't a threat, it's an opportunity. Trade is at the heart of the modern economy, and the prosperity it has generated. Trade is a key reason why hundreds of millions of people in China have been pulled out of poverty in recent decades, and why China's heft on the global stage again more closely matches its population size.

It is easy to take for granted the improvement in living standards. As we have seen, the oppressive forces of feudalism, colonialism and slavery once dominated the lives of many of the world's peoples. Psychologist Steven Pinker tells us that his favourite words are the encyclopedia entry that begins 'Smallpox *was* an infectious disease'.[3] Thanks to human progress, a disease that killed 500 million in its final century can now be referred to in the past tense.[4] Pinker notes that, due to better diets and more schooling, IQ scores have risen so rapidly that the average person today would score better than 98 per cent of the population a century ago. The odds of a typical European being murdered are less than one-tenth of what they would have been 500 years ago. Across the globe, attitudes on gender, race and sexuality have become more progressive, such that young Middle Eastern Muslims are about as tolerant as young Western Europeans were in the 1960s. Within a few generations, flush toilets, refrigerators, air conditioners and washing machines went from luxuries to necessities.

But has growth made us happier? In the 1970s, economist Richard Easterlin looked at early cross-national surveys of life satisfaction and concluded that beyond a certain point, more money did not make people any happier. The 'Easterlin Paradox' was accepted wisdom until the 2000s, when new analysis, based on much more extensive surveys, showed that it did not hold.[5] Within countries, people with higher incomes are happier. Across countries, people in nations with higher incomes are happier.

More than happiness, this new data shows that within and across countries, people with more income are more likely to say that they feel well rested, that they are treated with respect, that they smile and laugh a lot, and that they eat good-tasting food.[6] People with higher incomes – and people in nations with higher incomes – are less likely to say that they suffer physical pain, boredom or sadness. Within countries, people who have higher incomes are more likely to say that they experienced love. Sorry, Paul McCartney, money *can* buy you love.

While money continues to buy more happiness, the principle of diminishing marginal utility still holds. Increases in happiness seem roughly proportional to the percentage increase in income – meaning that a 10 per cent increase in income buys the same happiness boost to a homeless person as it does to a socialite. Yet that 10 per cent increase equates to many more dollars for someone who is rich than for someone who is poor. Consequently, the increase in inequality that has occurred in many nations over the past generation might have had an adverse impact on happiness. One of the best arguments for a redistributive welfare state and progressive taxation is that a dollar brings more pleasure to someone who does not have many dollars to begin with.

Income gaps between countries are even larger than those within countries. Western European incomes now average US$109 a day, while incomes in Latin America average only US$39 a day, and in Africa just US$10 a day.[7] The typical US resident produces almost as much output in a month as the average Nigerian does in a year. One factor driving growth in Africa is urbanisation, since people tend to be more productive when they move from a rural area to a city. Yet only half of the continent's population currently lives in towns and cities.[8] One reason is that African land ownership rights are often unclear, making people reluctant to invest in housing, and limiting the ability of city governments to raise property tax revenue. Sorting out land titling systems sounds mundane, but it will be fundamental to Africa's future prosperity.

The rise in inequality is not the only cause for economic concern. Research by economist George Akerlof on the economics of identity has highlighted the importance of considering how people perceive themselves. In the standard economic model, the only point of working is to earn income to consume. But the economics of identity reminds us that many people's identity is centred around what they produce, rather than what they consume. We are more likely to ask someone we've just met 'What do you do?' than 'What do you buy?' So when the twin forces of technology and trade have taken away factory jobs in advanced nations, it's cold comfort to tell the struggling middle class that televisions are getting cheaper. The rise of populist politicians is partly a backlash against the loss of secure working-class jobs, and a reminder of the importance of low unemployment to a stable society.

Since the Luddites, new technologies have been accompanied by frightening forecasts of job losses that have not eventuated. The latest challenge is posed by artificial intelligence. OpenAI's ChatGPT interface can debug computer code, write a corporate mission statement and summarise new scientific advances. 'GPT' stands for Generative Pre-trained Transformer, but it could also stand for general-purpose technology. Like coal-powered steam engines and electricity, artificial intelligence may ultimately be transformative. The widespread adoption of artificial intelligence is likely to boost average incomes, but many jobs could go the way of switchboard operators and lighthouse keepers. Economics reminds us that the cheaper a technology becomes, the more firms are likely to adopt it – with the biggest gains accruing to those who own the machines.

In the long run, artificial intelligence also represents a catastrophic risk to humanity.[9] At some point, intelligent machines are likely to outperform humans at all possible tasks. Not long after that, the gap between their abilities and ours will be like the gap between us and our household pets. When this happens, it will be crucial that these machines share our values and are willing to peacefully coexist with humanity.

An artwork showing the world's last selfie, produced by the author using artificial intelligence engine DALL·E.

Rogue artificial intelligence is probably the biggest long-term threat to humanity's future, but another key vulnerability comes from climate change. Economists talk about 'tail risk' – small chances of very bad outcomes. In the case of global warming, the tail risks come because we do not know how much carbon will be emitted in the future and how the planet will react to it. Further uncertainty comes from potential adverse feedback loops – such as the melting of the Greenland ice sheet or the loss of the Amazon rainforest. We know that climate change will be bad – but it could be very bad indeed.[10]

When facing small chances of catastrophe in our personal lives, economic thinking reminds us to buy insurance – paying a small annual premium to insure against the potential loss of our home, or the death of the primary income earner. Similarly, in the case of risks to humanity, we should spend a modest amount now on ethical artificial intelligence and cutting carbon emissions – as well as on reducing other existential risks, including bioterrorism and nuclear conflict.

Averting catastrophe will allow humanity to use the tools of economics to solve more prosaic problems. Due to traffic congestion, the average speed of traffic in London, Boston, Paris and Brussels is around 18 kilometres per hour (11 miles per hour), which is roughly the pace at which a horse might have trotted down those streets in the 1800s.[11] Traffic congestion costs the typical driver forty hours a year in Germany, fifty-one hours a year in the United States and eighty hours a year in the United Kingdom.[12] From Toronto to Mexico City, reducing traffic congestion would represent a major improvement in the quality of life for millions of city-dwellers.

WHAT'S THE WORST THAT COULD HAPPEN?

Much of the discussion around the risk of artificial intelligence focuses on 'bad' outcomes, including misinformation, algorithmic discrimination and the loss of jobs to automation. But another source of danger is the chance of catastrophe. Once artificial intelligence exceeds human intelligence, machines may accelerate away from us, as computers have done in board games such as chess and Go. Artificial intelligence would be humanity's last invention.

It is impossible to know what lies beyond that transition point, which scientists have dubbed 'the singularity'. Will the future look more like *Star Trek* or *Terminator*? Will productivity deliver lives of tranquillity to everyone, or will superintelligent machines decide that humanity is superfluous to their purposes?

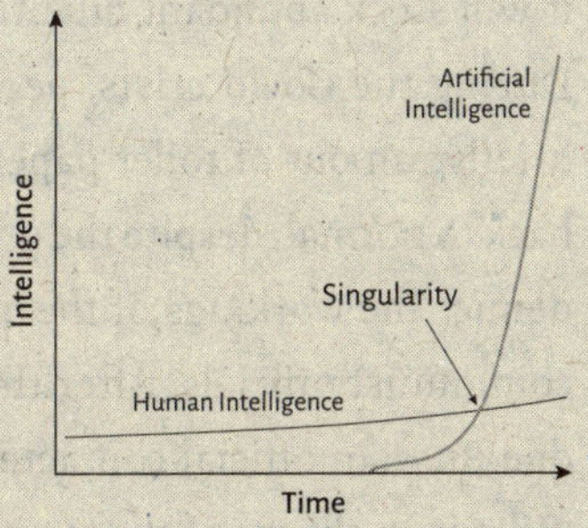

Economists who study uncertainty point out that it is useful to consider the full range of possibilities, not just the most likely. Economists use the notion of 'expected value', which involves multiplying the cost or benefit of an outcome by its probability. If there is a 1 per cent chance of winning $100 million, the expected value is $1 million. Similarly, the fair insurance premium for an item worth $100 million with a 1 per cent chance of loss would be $1 million.

A survey of expert artificial intelligence researchers finds that the median researcher expects the singularity to occur in 2059.[13] The median researcher says that there is a 5 per cent chance of an outcome that is 'Extremely bad (e.g. human extinction)'. Two-thirds of artificial intelligence researchers believe that society should place greater priority on artificial intelligence safety. In expected value terms, even small chances of disaster have large costs.

From a macroeconomic standpoint, a key frustration is that, nearly a century after the Great Depression, economists have failed to tame the boom-and-bust cycle. As a profession, we should be disappointed that modern economies still produce an economic crisis every decade or two. Crisis management is a significant part of the role of modern governments. Putting recessions in the rear-view mirror will mark a major achievement in economics.

Living in a capitalist economy, it is easy to take markets for granted. When we go to the supermarket, we assume that it will stock abundant quantities of every product we want. During the Covid crisis, people were shocked when stores briefly ran out of toilet paper. Within weeks, supplies were back to normal, despite the onset of a once-in-a-century pandemic. The workings of the 'invisible hand' once bewildered communist officials. After the breakup of the Soviet Union, one Russian official contacted a British economist, asking, 'Who is in charge of the supply of bread to the population of London?'[14] In the twenty-first century, the Russian and Chinese economies have transitioned from communism to capitalism, yet both are far from open democracies.

In 1946, US journalist Henry Hazlitt wrote *Economics in One Lesson*, the lesson being that market prices reflect opportunity costs. Seven decades later, the University of Queensland's John Quiggin wrote *Economics in Two Lessons*, the second lesson being that there is sometimes a wedge between market prices and true value. Hazlitt showed why markets foster growth, a key reason why capitalist economies have produced higher living standards than communist economies. Quiggin explained how markets can fail, producing pollution, unemployment and bullying monopolies. This book has told both sides of the story – how open markets have brought millions out of poverty, and why it is essential to address market failures for economies to prosper. Capitalism doesn't guarantee the wellbeing of those who lack capital.

One way to think about the role of government is as a risk manager: providing social insurance against risks as diverse as earthquakes, diseases and recessions. Standard government payments are not the only way to mitigate risk. Income-contingent loans – in which repayments only become due when the borrower's income passes a reasonable threshold – are used by some countries in place of college loans. Economists have suggested that income-contingent loans might also be used to provide assistance for drought-stricken farmers, struggling businesses or economically disadvantaged regions.[15]

The story of economics is also the tale of innovation. At the start of the twentieth century, the world had no planes, no radios and hardly any cars. By the end of the century, we surfed the internet on wifi-enabled laptops, flew on jet planes to meetings on the other side of the globe, and filled cities with skyscrapers. From air conditioners to antibiotics, barbed wire to the Haber-Bosch process, new technologies have reshaped our lives. Technologies have made markets work better too. One study found that when mobile phone service was introduced in the Indian fishing industry, prices converged and wastage was virtually eliminated.[16] Technology benefited consumers and producers alike.

Innovation rarely involves just the hard work of a lone genius.[17] Technological development isn't solely the work of Gutenberg, Curie, Edison, Lovelace, Gates, Jobs, Doudna and Musk. More commonly, technological breakthroughs occur in collaborative teams. The vacuum tube and the television depended on multiple firms, while a plethora of other innovations (including radar, the internet, germ theory, the pacemaker, magnetic resonance imaging and quantum mechanics) flowed out of non-market institutions such as government agencies and universities. Key technologies that power your smartphone – including GPS, voice-activated personal assistant and touchscreen display – were funded by government. At the heart of the economics of innovation is the question of how governments can continue to foster this kind of research.

Economics has practical advice for all aspects of life. Some stock-pickers claim that they can time their investing to sell at the peak and buy at the trough. Yet the evidence suggests that, rather than moving in predictable cycles, share prices follow a 'random walk'. Even John Maynard Keynes – the twentieth-century economist who did most to help smooth the business cycle – gave up on the idea of business cycle investing.[18]

At the outset, I said that this book aimed to do three things: tell the story of how capitalism and the market system emerged; discuss the key ideas and people who shaped the discipline of economics; and outline how economic forces have affected world history.

I hope that, in reading it, you see the history of humanity a little differently. When you look at a map of the world, recall how the shape of continents helped determine who colonised whom. When you see a mirror, think about how its invention created consumer culture. When you use a big tech platform, consider the way in which you are effectively paying with your data rather than with cash. Recognise your good fortune to live at a time when most of humanity has access to schools, vaccines and the internet.

The development of modern economics coincided with the industrial revolution, but it was not until the Great Depression that economists developed a deep understanding of the business cycle. Entranced by the efficiency of markets, early economists underestimated the ways in which market failure could occur, and were too quick to dismiss the role of government in making markets work better. More recent research has explored the dangers of monopolies and the risks of climate change. Behavioural economics is now a standard part of the curriculum, and the analysis of large datasets has become central to the work of many modern economists. Market designers have pioneered the matching algorithms that underpin many kidney donations. Auction experts have devised auctions that raise billions of dollars for government from the sale of electromagnetic spectrum rights. Development economists have run randomised trials that save lives and raise incomes.

Since most of us will not become economics researchers, the biggest contribution of economics is in helping us to live a better life. When making a tricky decision, weigh the costs and benefits. Consider the opportunity costs – what are you giving up? Think on the margin – asking whether one more of something is worth having. And don't forget externalities – the positive and negative impacts of your decisions on other people. From education to entrepreneurship, from socialising to the share market, economics can help you live a better life.

Acknowledgements

One of the best developments in modern economic scholarship is that an increasing share of research is co-authored. I have learned much of my economics from my collaborators and am grateful for the many conversations that have shaped our research and made me a better economist. Thanks too to my parliamentary colleagues – economists and non-economists – who have encouraged me to bring an economic perspective to our deliberations. At Black Inc., the team of Chris Feik, Kirstie Innes-Will and Jo Rosenberg have helped sharpen my arguments and shape my prose.

Jeff Borland, Paul Burke, Wendy Carlin, Bruce Chapman, Selwyn Cornish, Guido Erreygers, David Galenson, Joshua Gans, Ross Gittins, Bob Gregory, Nicholas Gruen, Dan Hamermesh, Tim Hatton, Richard Holden, Sebastian Leigh, Jan Libich, Xin Meng, Alex Millmow, Christine Neill, Alberto Posso, Adam Triggs and Justin Wolfers provided valuable comments on earlier drafts. Special thanks to my parents, Barbara and Michael Leigh, for their loving encouragement and detailed feedback.

This book is dedicated to my wife, Gweneth, and our three boys, Zachary, Theodore and Sebastian. I hope that you grow up in a society in which good economic policy internalises the externalities, the market gives you choices aplenty, and economics provides dazzling insights on our remarkable world.

Notes

INTRODUCTION

1. William Nordhaus, 1997, 'Do real-output and real-wage measures capture reality? The history of lighting suggests not' in William Nordhaus and Charles Hulten (eds), *The Economics of New Goods*, University of Chicago Press, Chicago, pp. 29–66.
2. The blending of microeconomics and macroeconomics has a long history. For a discussion of Paul Samuelson's 1948 Neoclassical Synthesis and the teaching of modern economics through the CORE curriculum, see Samuel Bowles and Wendy Carlin, 2020, 'What students learn in economics 101: Time for a change', *Journal of Economic Literature*, 58(1): 176–214.
3. Quoted in Avinash Dixit, 2014, *Microeconomics: A Very Short Introduction*, Oxford University Press, Oxford, p. 50.
4. Jeff Borland, 2008, *Microeconomics: Case Studies and Applications*, Cengage, Melbourne, p. 19.
5. Joshua Gans and Andrew Leigh, 2009, 'Born on the first of July: An (un) natural experiment in birth timing', *Journal of Public Economics*, 93.1–2: 246–63.
6. Wojciech Kopczuk and Joel Slemrod, 2003, 'Dying to save taxes: Evidence from estate-tax returns on the death elasticity', *Review of Economics and Statistics* 85(2): 256–65.
7. Lucy Black, 2020, 'Picking a product', *CKGSB Knowledge*, 19 November.
8. Benjamin Zhang, 2017, 'Trump just used Boeing's new global airliner to attack globalization', *Business Insider*, 18 February.
9. Thomas Thwaites, 2011, *The Toaster Project. Or A Heroic Attempt to Build a Simple Electric Appliance from Scratch*, Princeton Architectural Press, Princeton, NJ.
10. The median UK weekly wage in 2009 was around £490, or £19,000 for nine months. Thwaites's parts and travel totalled £1187. When I emailed him to check these figures, Thwaites wryly noted that my estimate of £20,000 was precisely the price at which he had sold the toaster to the V&A Museum.

1. OUT OF AFRICA AND INTO AGRICULTURE

1. Carina Schlebusch, Helena Malmström, Torsten Günther, Per Sjödin, et al., 2017, 'Southern African ancient genomes estimate modern human divergence to 350,000 to 260,000 years ago', *Science* 358(6363): 652–5.
2. Nicholas R. Longrich, 2020, 'When did we become fully human? What fossils and DNA tell us about the evolution of modern intelligence', *The Conversation*, 9 September.
3. David Baker, 2022, *The Shortest History of the World*, Black Inc., Melbourne, p. 110.
4. Caleb E. Finch, 2010, 'Evolution of the human lifespan and diseases of aging: Roles of infection, inflammation, and nutrition', *Proceedings of the National Academy of Sciences* 107, suppl 1: 1718–24.
5. Steven Pinker, 2011, *The Better Angels of Our Nature: Why Violence Has Declined*, Viking, New York. Another paper puts the figure at 2 per cent, which is still considerably higher than in modern times: Mark Pagel, 2016, 'Lethal violence deep in the human lineage', *Nature* 538(7624): 180–1.
6. Paul Salopek, 2018, 'Cities of silence', *National Geographic*, 31 August.
7. Ibid.
8. Hetalben Sindhav, 2016, 'The Indus Valley Civilisation (Harappan Civilisation)', *International Journal of Social Impact* 1(2): 69–75.
9. Philip Coggan, 2020, *More: A History of the World Economy from the Iron Age to the Information Age*, Hachette, New York, p. 26.
10. Jeremy Cherfas, 1989, 'Nuts to the desert', *New Scientist*, 19 August, pp. 44–7.
11. Melinda A. Zeder, 2011, 'The origins of agriculture in the Near East', *Current Anthropology* 52 (S4): S221–S235.
12. Shuanglei Wu, Yongping Wei, Brian Head, Yan Zhao and Scott Hann, 2019, 'The development of ancient Chinese agricultural and water technology from 8000 BC to 1911 AD', *Palgrave Communications* 5(1): 1–16.
13. Tim Harford, 2017, 'How the plough made the modern economy possible', BBC World Service, *50 Things That Made the Modern Economy*, 27 November.
14. James Burke, 1978, *Connections*, Macmillan, London, p. 12.
15. Alberto Alesina, Paola Giuliano and Nathan Nunn, 2013, 'On the origins of gender roles: Women and the plough', *Quarterly Journal of Economics* 128(2): 469–530.
16. François Pieter Retief and Louise Cilliers, 2006, 'Causes of death among the Caesars (27 BC – AD 476)' *Acta Theologica* 26(2): 89–106.

17. Average height went down from 5'10" (178 cm) for men and 5'6" (168 cm) for women to 5'5" (165 cm) and 5'1" (155 cm): Michael Hermanussen and Fritz Poustka, 2003, 'Stature of early Europeans', *Hormones* (Athens) 2(3): 175–8.
18. The difference between the short-term and long-term impacts of the agricultural revolution is why Jared Diamond is wrong to describe it as the worst mistake of the human race: Jared Diamond, 1999, 'The worst mistake in the history of the human race', *Discover Magazine*, 1 May. For example, without the agricultural revolution, it is unlikely that the world would have had the benefit of Diamond's brilliant writings.
19. Between the sixth and tenth centuries, watermills were widely adopted across Europe. By the time William the Conqueror carried out his 'Domesday Book' survey of England in 1086, he found an average of almost two watermills for every English village: Rondo Cameron, 1989, *A Concise Economic History of the World: From Paleolithic Times to the Present*, Oxford University Press, New York and Oxford, p. 71.
20. Laurence Iannaccone, 1998, 'Introduction to the economics of religion', *Journal of Economic Literature*, 36(3): 1465–95.
21. Pew Research Center, 2017, The Changing Global Religious Landscape, PEW Research Center, Washington DC.
22. Cameron, 1989, p. 83.
23. Donald Kagan, 1982, 'The dates of the earliest coins', *American Journal of Archaeology* 86(3): 343–60.
24. Neil Faulkner, 2012, *A Visitor's Guide to the Ancient Olympics*, Yale University Press, New Haven, CT, p. 126.
25. This estimate is based on edicts issued by Roman Emperor Diocletian, who ruled from 284 to 305 CE. See Coggan, 2020, p. 32.

2. THE GRAND CANAL, THE PRINTING PRESS AND THE PLAGUE

1. Cameron, 1989, p. 83.
2. Yiming Cao and Shuo Chen, 2022, 'Rebel on the canal: Disrupted trade access and social conflict in China, 1650–1911', *American Economic Review*, 112(5): 1555–90.
3. These figures are in 2011 US dollars and are drawn from Jutta Bolt and Jan Luiten van Zanden, 2020, 'Maddison style estimates of the evolution of the world economy. A new 2020 update', Maddison Project Database, University of Groningen, Groningen.

4. Niall Kishtainy, 2017, *A Little History of Economics*, Yale University Press, New Haven, p. 17.
5. Diego Puga and Daniel Trefler, 2014, 'International trade and institutional change: Medieval Venice's response to globalization', *Quarterly Journal of Economics* 129(2): 753–821.
6. Miles Corak, 2013, 'Inequality from generation to generation', in Robert Rycroft (ed.), *The Economics of Inequality, Poverty, and Discrimination in the 21st Century*, ABC-CLIO, Santa Barbara, CA, pp. 107–26.
7. Gregory Clark, 2014, *The Son Also Rises: Surnames and the History of Social Mobility*, Princeton University, Princeton, NJ.
8. Quoted in Tim Harford, 2006, *The Undercover Economist*, Oxford University Press, Oxford, pp. 201–2.
9. Masao Uchibayashi, 2006, 'Maize in pre-Columbian China found in Bencao Pinhui Jingyao', *Yakugaku Zasshi: Journal of the Pharmaceutical Society of Japan*, 126(1): 27–36.
10. Baker, 2022, p. 157.
11. Sascha O. Becker and Ludger Woessmann, 2009, 'Was Weber wrong? A human capital theory of Protestant economic history', *Quarterly Journal of Economics* 124(2): 531–96.
12. Coggan, 2020, p. 57.
13. Gary Anderson, Robert B. Ekelund, Robert F. Hebert and Robert D. Tollison, 1992, 'An economic interpretation of the medieval crusades', *Journal of European Economic History* 21(2): 339–63.
14. Coggan, 2020, pp. 7–8.
15. Şevket Pamuk, 2007, 'The Black Death and the origins of the "Great Divergence" across Europe, 1300–1600', *European Review of Economic History* 11(3): 289–317.

3. THE AGE OF SAIL

1. Trans-Atlantic Slave Trade Database, at slavevoyages.org.
2. The slavery statistics in this paragraph and the next are from David Baker, 2022, pp. 171–2.
3. 'Family separation among slaves in America was shockingly prevalent', *The Economist*, 18 June 2022.
4. Stephan Heblich, Stephen Redding and Hans-Joachim Voth, 2022, 'Slavery and the British Industrial Revolution', NBER Working Paper 30451, NBER, Cambridge, MA.

5. Carlos J. Charotti, Nuno Palma and João Pereira dos Santos, 2022, 'American treasure and the decline of Spain', Economics Discussion Paper Series EDP-2201, University of Manchester, Manchester.
6. Daron Acemoglu, Simon Johnson and James A. Robinson, 2001, 'The colonial origins of comparative development: An empirical investigation', *American Economic Review* 91(5): 1369–1401.
7. 'Armies of the East India Company', National Army Museum website, www.nam.ac.uk/explore/armies-east-india-company (undated).
8. John Brande Trend, 1957, *Portugal*, Praeger, New York, p. 103.
9. Emily Oster, 2004, 'Witchcraft, weather and economic growth in Renaissance Europe', *Journal of Economic Perspectives* 18(1): 215–28.
10. Peter Garber, 1990, 'Famous first bubbles', *Journal of Economic Perspectives*, 4(2): 35–54.

4. THE INDUSTRIAL REVOLUTION AND THE WEALTH OF NATIONS

1. These figures are in 2011 US dollars and are drawn from Bolt and Luiten van Zanden, 2020.
2. Gregory Clark, 2007, *A Farewell to Alms: A Brief Economic History of the World*, Princeton University Press, Princeton, NJ, p.38.
3. Bolt and Luiten van Zanden, 2020; Max Roser, Cameron Appel and Hannah Ritchie, 2013, 'Human height', available at ourworldindata.org/human-height.
4. Robert Allen, 2017, *The Industrial Revolution: A Very Short Introduction*, Oxford University Press, Oxford, pp. 4–7.
5. T.S. Ashton, 1948, *The Industrial Revolution 1760–1830*, Oxford University Press, Oxford, p. 42.
6. R.U. Ayres, 1989, *Technological Transformations and Long Waves*, International Institute for Applied Systems Analysis, Lazenburg, Austria, p. 17.
7. Nicholas Crafts, 2004, 'Steam as a general purpose technology: A growth accounting perspective', *Economic Journal* 114(49): 338–51.
8. Coggan, 2020, pp. 100–1.
9. Alexander C.R. Hammond, 2019, 'Heroes of progress, Pt. 13: James Watt', HumanProgress.org, 7 March.
10. Jesse Norman, 2018, *Adam Smith: What He Thought, and Why It Matters*, Penguin, London.
11. Todd Buchholz, 1999, *New Ideas from Dead Economists: An Introduction to Modern Economic Thought*, Penguin Books, London, p.14

12. Organisations such as the Polity Project and the Economist Intelligence Unit define full democracies as countries that respect civil liberties, have a democratic political culture and guarantee judicial independence and media freedom.
13. Ben Broadbent, 2020, 'Government debt and inflation', Bank of England speech, 2 September.
14. Mill's writings underlay the concept of '*Homo economicus*', although he did not use the term: see Joseph Persky, 1995, 'Retrospectives: The ethology of homo economicus', *Journal of Economic Perspectives* 9(2): 221–31.
15. Steven Johnson, 2014, *How We Got to Now: Six Inventions That Made the Modern World*, Riverhead Books, New York, p. 32.
16. E.P. Thompson, 1967, 'Work–discipline, and industrial capitalism', *Past and Present* 38: 56–97.
17. John Brown, 1990, 'The condition of England and the standard of living: Cotton textiles in the northwest, 1806–1850', *Journal of Economic History* 50(3): 591–614.
18. Joshua Gans and Andrew Leigh, 2019, *Innovation + Equality: How to Create a Future That Is More Star Trek Than Terminator*, MIT Press, Cambridge, MA, p. 24.
19. J.A. Schumpeter, 1954, *History of Economic Analysis*, Oxford University Press, New York, p. 500.
20. Wolfgang Keller and Carol H. Shiue, 2020, 'China's foreign trade and investment, 1800–1950', NBER Working Paper 27558, NBER, Cambridge, MA.
21. Allen, 2017, p. 97.
22. Steven Pressman, 1999, *Fifty Major Economists*, Routledge, London, p. 36.
23. Quoted in Kishtainy, 2017, p. 40.

5. TRADE, TRAVEL AND TECHNOLOGY TAKE OFF

1. Mr Cobden, 1965, *The Collected Works of Walter Bagehot*, Norman St John-Stevas (ed.), vol. 3, p. 216.
2. A.C. Howe, 2008, 'Anti-Corn Law League', *Oxford Dictionary of National Biography* [online resource].
3. Allen, 2017, p. 119.
4. United Nations Office on Drugs and Crime, 2008, *World Drug Report 2008*, United Nations, New York, p. 175.

5. This discussion of Japan's economic development draws on Allen, 2017, pp. 119–24.
6. Cameron, 1989, pp. 275–6.
7. Richard Baldwin, 2006, 'Globalisation: The great unbundling(s)', Prime Minister's Office, Economic Council of Finland.
8. Bolt and Luiten van Zanden, 2020.
9. Allen, 2017, p. 76.
10. From 'Our World in Data', at ourworldindata.org/grapher/cross-country-literacy-rates.
11. Matthew J. Gallman, 1994, *The North Fights the Civil War: The Home Front*, Ivan R. Dee, Chicago, p. 95.
12. David Galenson, 2006, *Old Masters and Young Geniuses: The Two Cycles of Artistic Creativity*, Princeton University Press, Princeton, NJ.
13. Sophia Twarog, 1997, 'Heights and living standards in Germany, 1850–1939: The case of Wurttemberg' in Richard H. Steckel and Roderick Floud (eds), *Health and Welfare During Industrialization*, University of Chicago Press, Chicago, pp. 285–330.
14. Peter Dunn, 2002, 'Stéphane Tarnier (1828–97), the architect of perinatology in France', *Archives of Disease in Childhood: Fetal and Neonatal Edition* 86(2): F137–9.
15. Geoff Boeing, 2019, 'Urban spatial order: Street network orientation, configuration, and entropy', *Applied Network Science* 4(1): 1–19.

6. ECONOMIC MODELS AND THE MODERN FACTORY

1. Thomas M. Humphrey, 1992, 'Marshallian cross diagrams and their uses before Alfred Marshall: The origins of supply and demand geometry', *Economic Review*, 78: 3–23.
2. Henry Ford and Samuel Crowther, 1922, *My Life and Work*, Garden City Publishing Company, Garden City, New York, p. 72.
3. Coggan, 2020, p. 156.
4. See, for example, 'Say drug habit grips the nation', *The New York Times*, 5 December 1913, p. 8.
5. Tim Hatton, personal communication.
6. Niall Ferguson, 2008, *The Ascent of Money: A Financial History of the World*, Penguin, New York, p.186.

7. Stephen Broadberry and Mark Harrison (eds), 2005, *The Economics of World War I*, Cambridge University Press, Cambridge, UK. The calculation is for 1914, so the Allied powers include Russia (which would later drop out) but exclude powers that joined later (such as Italy and the United States).
8. Andrei Markevich and Mark Harrison, 2011, 'Great War, Civil War, and recovery: Russia's national income, 1913 to 1928', *Journal of Economic History* 71(3): 672–703.
9. George Rose and Sherrylynn Rowe, 2015, 'Northern cod comeback', *Canadian Journal of Fisheries and Aquatic Sciences* 72, no. 12: 1789–98.

7. WORLD WAR I AND THE DEPRESSION

1. Broadberry and Harrison, 2005, p.28.
2. An outcome predicted by John Maynard Keynes, 1919, *The Economic Consequences of the Peace*, Macmillan, London.
3. Coggan, 2020, p. 181.
4. Paul Krugman, 1998, 'The hangover theory', *Slate*, 4 December.
5. Bruce Caldwell and Hansjoerg Klausinger, 2022, *Hayek: A Life 1899–1950*, University of Chicago Press, Chicago.
6. Kishtainy, 2017, p. 104.
7. Richard Davenport-Hines, 2015, *Universal Man: The Seven Lives of John Maynard Keynes*, William Collins, London, p. 214.
8. Lionel Robbins, 1971, *Autobiography of an Economist*, Palgrave, London, p. 154.
9. Walter Galenson and Arnold Zellner, 1957, 'International comparison of unemployment rates' in *The Measurement and Behavior of Unemployment*, NBER, Cambridge, MA, pp. 439–584. Some recent studies differ slightly – for example putting Australia above 10 per cent and the UK just below 10 per cent. In 1939, US unemployment also exceeded 10 per cent: see fred.stlouisfed.org/series/M0892AUSM156SNBR.
10. The examples of how tariffs hurt domestic production are drawn from Alan Reynolds, 1979, 'What do we know about the Great Crash?' *National Review*, 9 November.
11. The examples of retaliatory trade measures in this paragraph are drawn from Kris James Mitchener, Kevin Hjortshøj O'Rourke and Kirsten Wandschneider, 2022, 'The Smoot-Hawley trade war', *Economic Journal* 132(647): 2500–33.
12. The examples of immigration restrictions in this paragraph are drawn from Joseph Ferrie and Timothy Hatton, 2015, 'Two centuries

of international migration', *Handbook of the Economics of International Migration*, 1: 53–88.

13. See, for example, Nick Freeman, 2002, 'Foreign direct investment in Cambodia, Laos and Vietnam: A regional overview', Paper prepared for the Conference on Foreign Direct Investment: Opportunities and Challenges for Cambodia, Laos and Vietnam, 16–17 August, Hanoi.
14. Sadie Alexander (ed. Nina Banks), 2021, *Democracy, Race, and Justice: The Speeches and Writings of Sadie T. M. Alexander*, Yale Press, New Haven, CT; 'Economists are rediscovering a lost heroine', *The Economist*, 19 December 2020.
15. Manuel Funke, Moritz Schularick and Christoph Trebesch, 2016, 'Going to extremes: Politics after financial crises, 1870–2014', *European Economic Review* 88, 227–60.

8. WORLD WAR II AND BRETTON WOODS

1. For more detail, see Coggan, 2020, p. 198.
2. The economic comparisons of World War II are drawn from Mark Harrison, 1998, *The Economics of World War II: Six Great Powers in International Comparison*, Cambridge University Press, Cambridge, UK. The calculation is for 1938, so includes the Allied countries that would be lost (Poland, Czechoslovakia, France and its empire), while excluding nations that would later join the Allied side (the Soviet Union and the United States).
3. J. Bradford DeLong, 2023, *Slouching Towards Utopia: An Economic History of the Twentieth Century*, Hachette, New York, p. 304.
4. Phillips Payson O'Brien, 2015, *How the War Was Won: Air-Sea Power and Allied Victory in World War II*, Cambridge University Press, Cambridge, UK.
5. Harrison, 1998.
6. J. Bradford DeLong and Barry Eichengreen, 1993, 'The Marshall Plan: History's most successful structural adjustment program' in Rudiger Dornbusch, Wilhelm Nolling and Richard Layard (eds), *Postwar Economic Reconstruction and Lessons for the East Today*, MIT Press, Cambridge, MA, pp. 189–230.
7. Selwyn Cornish and Alex Millmow, 2016, 'A.W.H. Phillips and Australia', *History of Economics Review* 63(1): 2–20.
8. Vito Tanzi and Ludger Schuknecht, 2000, *Public Spending in the 20th century: A Global Perspective*, Cambridge University Press, Cambridge, UK, p. 6.

9. THE GLORIOUS THIRTY?

1. Branko Milanović, 2008, 'Where in the world are you? Assessing the importance of circumstance and effort in a world of different mean country incomes and (almost) no migration', Policy Research Working Paper 4493, World Bank, Washington, DC.
2. OECD, 2019, *Negotiating Our Way Up: Collective Bargaining in a Changing World of Work*, OECD, Paris.
3. Jan Tinbergen, 1974, 'Substitution of graduate by other labour', *Kyklos* 27(2): 217–26; Claudia Goldin and Lawrence Katz, 2008, *The Race Between Education and Technology*, Harvard University Press, Cambridge, MA.
4. Andrew Stanley, 2022, *Global Inequalities*, International Monetary Fund, Washington, DC.
5. Andrew Leigh, 2009, 'Does the world economy swing national elections?', *Oxford Bulletin of Economics and Statistics* 71(2): 163–81.
6. Alan Holmans, 2005, *Historical Statistics of Housing in Britain*, Cambridge Centre for Housing & Planning Research, University of Cambridge, Cambridge, UK, pp. 130, 143.
7. Steven Johnson, 2010, *Where Good Ideas Come From: The Natural History of Innovation*, Penguin, New York, pp. 214–15.
8. Kishtainy, 2017, p. 134.
9. Gary Becker, 1968, 'Crime and punishment: An economic approach', *Journal of Political Economy*, 76(2): 169–217.
10. Gary Becker, 1957, *The Economics of Discrimination*, University of Chicago Press, Chicago.
11. These figures are post-Brexit.
12. Air Transport Association of America, 1970, *1970 Air Transport Facts and Figures*, ATAA, Washington, DC.
13. 'Credit card debt statistics', available at balancingeverything.com/credit-card-debt-statistics/, updated 6 January 2023.
14. Anja Achtziger, 2022, 'Overspending, debt, and poverty', *Current Opinion in Psychology*: 101342.
15. George Akerlof, 1970, 'The market for lemons: Quality uncertainty and the market mechanism', *Quarterly Journal of Economics* 84(3): 488–500.
16. David Card and Stefano DellaVigna, 2013, 'Nine facts about top journals in economics', *Journal of Economic Literature* 51(1): 144–61.
17. Coggan, 2020, pp. 234–5.

18. Author's calculations, based on Bolt and Luiten van Zanden, 2020.
19. Helen Yaffe, 2009, *Che Guevara: The Economics of Revolution*, Palgrave Macmillan, London, p. 21.
20. Gordon Corera, 'India: The economy', BBC, 3 December 1998.
21. Marco Colagrossi, Domenico Rossignoli and Mario A. Maggioni. 2020, 'Does democracy cause growth? A meta-analysis (of 2000 regressions)', *European Journal of Political Economy* 61: 101824.
22. MV Lee Badgett, Sheila Nezhad, Kees Waaldijk and Yana van der Meulen Rodgers, 2014, 'The relationship between LGBT inclusion and economic development: An analysis of emerging economies', Williams Institute and US AID, Washington, DC.
23. Aniruddha Mitra, James T. Bang and Arnab Biswas, 2015, 'Gender equality and economic growth: Is it equality of opportunity or equality of outcomes?', *Feminist Economics* 21(1): 110–35.
24. Angus Maddison, 2006, *The World Economy*. OECD, Paris, p. 178.
25. Author's calculations, based on Bolt and Luiten van Zanden, 2020.
26. Cormac Ó Gráda, 2007, 'Making famine history', *Journal of Economic Literature*, 45(1): 5–38.

10. MARKETS, MARKETS EVERYWHERE

1. Ke Wang, 2008, 'Xiaogang Village, birthplace of rural reform, moves on', China.org.cn, 15 December.
2. This account is largely drawn from David Kestenbaum and Jacob Goldstein, 2012, 'The secret document that transformed China', *Planet Money*, 20 January.
3. Nicholas Lardy, 2016, 'The changing role of the private sector in China' in Iris Day and John Simon (eds), *Structural Change in China: Implications for Australia and the World*, Reserve Bank of Australia, Sydney, pp. 37–50.
4. Shujie Yao, 2000, 'Economic development and poverty reduction in China over 20 years of reforms', *Economic Development and Cultural Change* 48(3): 447–74.
5. Julia Simon and Kenny Malone, 2021, 'Looking back on when President Reagan fired the air traffic controllers', *NPR Morning Edition*, 5 August.
6. William A. Niskanen, 1988, *Reaganomics: An Insider's Account of the Policies and the People*, Oxford University Press, Oxford.
7. Mark Carney, 2021, *Value(s): Building a Better World for All*, William Collins, London, p. 173.

8. William L. Megginson and Jeffry M. Netter, 2001, 'From state to market: A survey of empirical studies on privatization', *Journal of Economic Literature* 39(2): 321-389..
9. Michael Porter, 1979, 'How competitive forces shape strategy', *Harvard Business Review* 57: 137-145.
10. Daniel Hamermesh, 2011, *Beauty Pays: Why Attractive People Are More Successful*, Princeton University Press, Princeton, NJ.

11. INFLATION TARGETING AND INEQUALITY

1. Coggan, 2020, p. 224.
2. '$100 billion for three eggs', *Herald Sun*, 25 July 2008.
3. Coggan, 2020, p. 258.
4. Gerald Bouey, governor of the Bank of Canada, speaking in 1982.
5. Kenneth Rogoff, 2022, 'The age of inflation', *Foreign Affairs*, Nov/Dec.
6. William McChesney Martin Jr, 1955, 'Address before the New York Group of Investment Bankers Association of America', 19 October.>
7. 'One more push', *The Economist*, 21 July 2011.
8. Facundo Alvaredo, Lucas Chancel, Thomas Piketty, Emmanuel Saez and Gabriel Zucman, 2017, *World Inequality Report 2018*, Paris School of Economics, Paris, pp. 123–30.
9. World Bank, Doing Business project, available at www.worldbank.org/en/programs/business-enabling-environment/doing-business-legacy (the project was discontinued in 2021).
10. Douglas Irwin, 2022, 'The trade reform wave of 1985–1995', *AEA Papers and Proceedings*, 112: 244–51.
11. Chad Bown and Douglas Irwin, 2015, 'The GATT's starting point: Tariff levels circa 1947', NBER Working Paper 21782; World Bank, 'Tariff rate, applied, weighted mean, all products (%)', available at data.worldbank.org/indicator/TM.TAX.MRCH.WM.AR.ZS.
12. Bolt and Luiten van Zanden, 2020.
13. See, for example, Justin Yifu Lin, 2019, 'New structural economics: The third generation of development economics', GEGI Working Paper 27, Global Development Policy Center, Boston University, Boston.
14. Mariana Mazzucato, 2013. *The Entrepreneurial State: Debunking Public vs. Private Myths in Risk and Innovation*, Anthem Press, London.
15. 'India's population will start to shrink sooner than expected', *The*

Economist, 2 December 2021.

16. United Nations Department of Economic and Social Affairs, Population Division, 2022. *World Population Prospects 2022*, United Nations, New York.
17. Steven Ritter, 2008, 'The Haber–Bosch reaction: An early chemical impact on sustainability', *Chemical and Engineering News* 86(33).
18. Stuart Smyth, 2020, 'The human health benefits from GM crops', *Plant Biotechnology Journal* 18(4): 887–8.
19. Abdul Latif Jameel Poverty Action Lab (J-PAL), 2018, 'Free bednets to fight malaria', J-PAL Evidence to Policy Case Study.
20. Facundo Alvaredo, Lucas Chancel, Thomas Piketty, Emmanuel Saez and Gabriel Zucman, 2017, *World Inequality Report 2018*, Paris School of Economics, Paris, pp. 113–22.
21. For a longer discussion of this point, see Gans and Leigh, 2019.
22. William Kissick, 1994, *Medicine's Dilemmas: Infinite Needs Versus Finite Resources*, Yale University Press, New Haven, CT.
23. These examples are drawn from David Cutler and Mark McClellan, 2001, 'Is technological change in medicine worth it?', *Health Affairs* 20(5): 11–29.
24. John Kenneth Galbraith, 1958, *The Affluent Society*, Houghton Mifflin Company, Boston.
25. The Business Research Company, 2023, *Sports Global Market Report 2023*, The Business Research Company, London.
26. Joseph Price and Justin Wolfers, 2010, 'Racial discrimination among NBA referees', *Quarterly Journal of Economics*, 125(4): 1859–87.
27. Kai Fischer, J. James Reade and W. Benedikt Schmal, 2022, 'What cannot be cured must be endured: The long-lasting effect of a Covid-19 infection on workplace productivity', *Labour Economics* 79, 102281.
28. Graham Kendall and Liam Lenten, 2017, 'When sports rules go awry', *European Journal of Operational Research* 257(2): 377–94.

12. HOT MARKETS AND A HOTTER PLANET

1. See www.internetworldstats.com/emarketing.htm.
2. In recent years, malaria deaths have averaged around 600,000 (World Health Organization World Malaria Report), while shark deaths have averaged around seventy (Florida Museum of Natural History's International Shark Attack File). Motor vehicle fatalities have averaged

around 1.3 million (World Health Organization), while aviation fatalities have averaged around 300 (Aviation Safety Network).

3. Daniel Kahneman, 2011, *Thinking, Fast and Slow*, Farrar, Straus and Giroux, New York.

4. OECD, 2022, 'HM 1.2 House Prices', OECD Affordable Housing Database, OECD, Paris.

5. Shiller's 2007 rollercoaster simulation can be viewed at www.youtube.com/watch?v=kUldGc06S3U.

6. Michael Lewis, 2010, *The Big Short: Inside the Doomsday Machine*, WW Norton, New York.

7. International Labour Organization, 2018, *Global Wage Report 2018/19: What Lies Behind Gender Pay Gaps*, ILO, Geneva.

8. Doris Weichselbaumer and Rudof Winter-Ebmer, 2005, 'A meta-analysis on the international gender wage gap', *Journal of Economic Surveys* 19 (3): 479–511.

9. Alexandra de Pleijt and Jan Luiten van Zanden, 2021, 'Two worlds of female labour: gender wage inequality in western Europe, 1300–1800', *Economic History Review* 74 (3): 611–38.

10. Kristen Schilt and Matthew Wiswall, 2008, 'Before and after: Gender transitions, human capital, and workplace experiences', *BE Journal of Economic Analysis & Policy* 8(1).

11. Claudia Goldin, 2021, *Career and Family: Women's Century-Long Journey Toward Equity*, Princeton University Press, Princeton, NJ.

12. Rick Glaubitz, Astrid Harnack-Eber and Miriam Wetter, 2022, 'The gender gap in lifetime earnings: The role of parenthood', DIW Berlin Discussion Paper 2001, DIW, Berlin; Fatih Guvenen, Greg Kaplan, Jae Song and Justin Weidner, 2022, 'Lifetime earnings in the United States over six decades', *American Economic Journal: Applied Economics* 14(4): 446–79.

13. Jhacova Williams, 'Laid off more, hired less: Black workers in the Covid-19 recession', RAND blog, 29 September 2020.

14. Robert Klitgaard, 1988, *Controlling Corruption*, University of California Press, Oakland, CA.

15. Annette Alstadsæter, Niels Johannesen and Gabriel Zucman, 2018, 'Who owns the wealth in tax havens? Macro evidence and implications for global inequality', *Journal of Public Economics* 162: 89–100.

16. Seema Jayachandran and Michael Kremer, 2006, 'Odious debt', *American Economic Review* 96(1): 82–92.

17. Tim Harford, 2020, *How to Make the World Add Up: Ten Rules for Thinking Differently About Numbers*, Little, Brown Book Group, London.
18. See www.guinnessworldrecords.com/world-records/most-successful-chimpanzee-on-wall-street.
19. Tim Edwards, Anu R. Ganti, Craig Lazzara, Joseph Nelesen and Davide Di Gioia, 2022, 'SPIVA U.S. Mid-Year 2022', S&P Dow Jones Indices, New York, p. 7.
20. Alexander Chinco and Marco Sammon, 2022, 'The passive-ownership share is double what you think it is', available at ssrn.com/abstract=4188052.
21. Annie Lowrey, 2021, 'Could index funds be "worse than Marxism"?', *The Atlantic*, 5 April.
22. IGM Economic Experts Panel, 2019, 'Diversified investing', Initiative on Global Markets, Chicago Booth, Chicago, 28 January.
23. Tyler Cowen, 2011, *The Great Stagnation: How America Ate All the Low-Hanging Fruit of Modern History, Got Sick, and Will (Eventually) Feel Better*, Dutton, New York.
24. Andrew G Haldane, 2015, 'Stuck', Speech given at the Open University, Milton Keynes, 30 June.
25. See the Atlantic Council's 'Global QE Tracker', available at www.atlanticcouncil.org/global-qe-tracker/.
26. Steve Liesman, 2019, 'Trump's tariffs are equivalent to one of the largest tax increases in decades', *CNBC*, 16 May.
27. Joseph Francois, Laura Baughman and Daniel Anthony, 2018, 'Round 3: "Trade discussion" or "trade war"? The estimated impacts of tariffs on steel and aluminum', Trade Partnership, Washington, DC, 5 June.
28. Pablo Fajgelbaum, Pinelopi Goldberg, Patrick Kennedy and Amit Khandelwal, 2020, 'The return to protectionism', *Quarterly Journal of Economics* 135(1): 1–55.
29. 'Impact of Brexit on economy "worse than Covid"', *BBC News*, 27 October 2021.

13. THE PANDEMIC AND BEYOND

1. Rakesh Padhan and K.P. Prabheesh, 2021, 'The economics of Covid-19 pandemic: A survey', *Economic Analysis and Policy* 70: 220–37.
2. Padhan and Prabheesh, 2021.
3. International Monetary Fund, 2022, *2022 Global Debt Monitor*, IMF, Washington, DC, p. 7.

4. See, for example, Centers for Disease Control and Prevention, 2021, 'Morbidity and mortality weekly report' 70(37), 17 September.
5. Evan P. Starr, James J. Prescott and Norman D. Bishara, 2021, 'Noncompete agreements in the US labor force', *Journal of Law and Economics* 64(1): 53–84.
6. Amy Webb, 2019, *The Big Nine: How the Tech Titans and Their Thinking Machines Could Warp Humanity*, Public Affairs, New York.
7. Hannah Fry, 2018, *Hello World: Being Human in the Age of Algorithms*, WW Norton, London.
8. Cathy O'Neil, 2016, *Weapons of Math Destruction*, Crown, New York.
9. Shoshana Zuboff, 2019, *The Age of Surveillance Capitalism: The Fight for a Human Future at the New Frontier of Power*, Profile Books, New York.
10. Raj Chetty, David Grusky, Maximilian Hell, Nathaniel Hendren, Robert Manduca and Jimmy Narang, 2017, 'The fading American dream: Trends in absolute income mobility since 1940', *Science* 356(6336): 398–406; Raj Chetty and Nathaniel Hendren, 2018, 'The effects of neighborhoods on intergenerational mobility I: Childhood exposure effects', *Quarterly Journal of Economics* 133(3): 1107–62; Raj Chetty and Nathaniel Hendren, 2018, 'The effects of neighborhoods on intergenerational mobility II: County level estimates', *Quarterly Journal of Economics* 133(3): 1163–1228.
11. Raj Chetty, Matthew O. Jackson, Theresa Kuchler, Johannes Stroebel et al., 2022, 'Social Capital I: Measurement and Associations with Economic Mobility', *Nature* 608(7921): 108–21; Raj Chetty, Matthew O. Jackson, Theresa Kuchler, Johannes Stroebel et al., 2022, 'Social Capital II: Determinants of Economic Connectedness', *Nature* 608(7921): 122–34.
12. All forensic economics examples are from Eric Zitzewitz, 2012, 'Forensic economics', *Journal of Economic Literature*, 50(3): 731–69.
13. The research was ultimately published as Andrew Leigh, 2010, 'Who benefits from the earned income tax credit? Incidence among recipients, coworkers and firms', *BE Journal of Economic Analysis and Policy* 10(1).
14. Seth Stephens-Davidowitz, 2017, *Everybody Lies: What the Internet Can Tell Us About Who We Really Are*, Bloomsbury, London.
15. Hoyt Bleakley and Jeffrey Lin, 2012, 'Portage and path dependence', *Quarterly Journal of Economics* 127(2): 587–644.
16. Luis Martinez, 2022, 'How much should we trust the dictator's GDP growth estimates?' *Journal of Political Economy* 130(10): 2731–69.

17. These examples and many more are summarised in Dave Donaldson and Adam Storeygard, 2016, 'The view from above: Applications of satellite data in economics', *Journal of Economic Perspectives* 30(4): 171–98.
18. Erik Brynjolfsson, Avinash Collis and Felix Eggers, 2019, 'Using massive online choice experiments to measure changes in well-being', *Proceedings of the National Academy of Sciences* 116(15): 7250–5.
19. Kishtainy, 2017, pp. 208–9.
20. Marilyn Waring, 1988, *If Women Counted: A New Feminist Economics*. Harper and Row, San Francisco.

14. ECONOMICS: PAST, PRESENT AND FUTURE

1. Max Roser, 2016, 'Stop saying that 2016 was the "worst year"', *The Washington Post*, 29 December.
2. Child mortality figures from ourworldindata.org/child-mortality (for early 1970s) and childmortality.org (for 2021, the most recent year available at the time of writing). Services employment figures from World Bank (indicator SL.SRV.EMPL.ZS).
3. Steven Pinker, 2018, *Enlightenment Now: The Case for Reason, Science, Humanism, and Progress*, Viking, New York.
4. On the death toll from smallpox, see Donald Henderson, 2009, *Smallpox: The Death of a Disease*, Prometheus Books, Amherst, New York, p. 12.
5. Betsey Stevenson and Justin Wolfers. 2008, 'Economic growth and happiness: Reassessing the Easterlin paradox', *Brookings Papers on Economic Activity*, Spring 2008, pp. 1–87; Angus Deaton, 2008, 'Income, health, and well-being around the world: Evidence from the Gallup World Poll', *Journal of Economic Perspectives* 22(2), pp. 53–72.
6. Stevenson and Wolfers, 2008.
7. The daily income estimates in this paragraph are from Bolt and Luiten van Zanden, 2020.
8. OECD/SWAC, 2020, *Africa's Urbanisation Dynamics 2020: Africapolis, Mapping a New Urban Geography*, West African Studies, OECD Publishing, Paris.
9. For more on catastrophic risk, see Andrew Leigh, 2021, *What's the Worst That Could Happen? Existential Risk and Extreme Politics*, MIT Press, Cambridge, MA.
10. Gernot Wagner and Martin L. Weitzman, 2016, *Climate Shock: The Economic Consequences of a Hotter Planet*, Princeton University Press, Princeton NJ.
11. Bob Pishue, 2023, *2022 INRIX Global Traffic Scorecard*, INRIX, Kirkland, WA.

12. Pishue, 2023.
13. Zach Stein-Perlman, Benjamin Weinstein-Raun and Katja Grace, '2022 expert survey on progress in AI', AI Impacts, 3 August 2022, https://aiimpacts.org/2022-expert-survey-on-progress-in-ai/.
14. Coggan, 2020, p. 357.
15. Bruce Chapman (ed.), 2006, *Government Managing Risk: Income Contingent Loans for Social and Economic Progress*, Routledge, London.
16. Robert Jensen, 2007, 'The digital provide: Information (technology), market performance, and welfare in the South Indian fisheries sector', *Quarterly Journal of Economics* 122(3): 879–924.
17. The discussion in this paragraph draws on Johnson, 2010, pp. 230, 236.
18. Harford, 2020, p. 273.

Image Credits

p. 1: P. Maxwell Photography / Shutterstock.

p. 2: Vladimir Gjorgiev / Shutterstock.

p. 14: Courtesy of Archestudy.

p. 17: Jared Diamond. Image via Wikimedia Commons.

p. 21: IR Stone / Shutterstock.

p. 24: Image via r / ArtefactPorn, Reddit.

p. 29: Mary Long and Holaillustrations / Shutterstock.

p. 33: Unknown artist, c. 1665. Image via Wikimedia Commons.

p. 38: Workshop of Bronzino, Portrait of Lorenzo the Magnificent, c. 1565–69, Uffizi Gallery. Image via Wikimedia Commons.

p. 41: Duncan1890 / iStockPhoto.

p. 44: Unknown artist, c. 1640, Norton Simon Art Foundation. Image via Wikimedia Commons.

p. 47: James Watt's Patent via itakehistory.com.

p. 51: Heritage Image Partnership Ltd / Alamy Stock Photo.

p. 55: Working Class Movement Library catalogue. Image via Wikimedia Commons.

p. 56: Chronicle / Alamy Stock Photo.

p. 61: Watercolour by Richard Simkin held in the Anne S.K. Brown Military Collection, Brown University. Image via Wikimedia Commons.

p. 67: Photograph by Carl Van Vechten, 13 November 1948, Van Vechten Collection at Library of Congress. Image via Wikimedia Commons.

p. 69: Chronicle / Alamy Stock Photo.

p. 71: The Landlord's Game, designed by Lizzie J. Magie (Phillips), published in 1906 by the Economic Game Company, New York. Image: Thomas Forsyth.

p. 78: Photographer unknown, Henry Ford Interview, *Literary Digest*, 1 July 1928. Image via Wikimedia Commons.

p. 79: Martin Forstenzer / Hulton Archive / Getty.

p. 80: Mpv_51. Image via Wikimedia Commons.

p. 83: © Holger Motzkau 2010. Image via Wikimedia Commons.

p. 85: Pictorial Press / Alamy Stock Photo.

p. 87: Fotosearch / Stringer / Getty Images.

p. 93: Library of Congress Prints and Photographs Division Washington. Image via Wikimedia Commons.

p. 96: Unknown photographer, c. June 1921. Image via Wikimedia Commons.

p. 100: Artwork by Trevor Bragdon / *Pitch + Persuade*.

p. 102: From 'The Phillips Machine Project' by Nicholas Barr, *LSE Magazine*, June 1988, no. 75, p.3. Image via Wikimedia Commons.

p. 108: People's History Museum.

p. 111: Carol M. Highsmith Archive, Library of Congress. Image via Wikimedia Commons.

p. 114: apiguide / Shutterstock.

p. 115: Fig. 2 taken from Kathryn Cardarelli and Rachael S. Jackson, *Education Policy as Health Promotion*, white paper presented at the First Annual Conference of the J. McDonald Williams Institute in Dallas, Texas, in October 2005.

p. 121: Bettmann / Getty Images.

p. 123: Illustrated London News, 22 December 1849. Image via Wikimedia Commons.

p. 131: Art_Photo / Shutterstock.

p. 136: Graph by Alan Laver based on 'Inflation and central bank independence: OECD countries', Our World in Data.

p. 147: Graph by Alan Laver, based on Fig. 2, *World Inequality Report 2018*, compiled by Facundo Alvaredo, Lucas Chancel, Thomas Piketty, Emmanuel Saez and Gabriel Zucman, presented at the Paris School of Economics.

p. 150: Caio Pederneiras / Shutterstock.

p. 151: Alex Bogatyrev / Shutterstock.

p. 158: CP PHOTO / Troy Fleece.

p. 160: ©Johan Jarnestad/The Royal Swedish Academy of Sciences.

p. 178: Leonard Zhukovsky / Shutterstock.

p. 187: DALL-E, used under an Open AI Responsible Licence.

Index

Page numbers in **bold** refer to images.